Thank You!

Rick McC[illegible]

Mk. 5:19

DEAFCHURCH 21

Vision for a New Generation

Bob Ayres and Rick McClain

Ayres & McClain
PUBLISHING

Excellence in Deaf Ministry Books

Deafchurch 21

Vision for a New Generation

Bob Ayres and Rick McClain

A&M Publishing

Louisville, Kentucky

ISBN (Print Edition): 978-1-54397-959-6

ISBN (eBook Edition): 978-1-54397-960-2

DEAFCHURCH 21: Vision for a New Generation

Deaf churches and ministries today face a crisis in reaching Deaf and hard of hearing young people. As the end of the twentieth century approached, we stood at the brink of a dispersed and completely secularized Deaf culture. The influence and impact of the Christian faith—any religious belief system for that matter—had been greatly diminished. Fortunately, this is not the end of the story.

With the advent of the twenty-first century, a renewed, growing spirit of spirituality and unity spread across the Deaf community, particularly among youth and young adults, that resulted in what could be described as a revival like one not seen in decades. The question in this book is presented and addressed: what are the essential principles for ministry with and to this next generation?

We live in a highly secularized and urbanized society that is both divided and united by media and technology. In DEAFCHURCH 21, challenges, essential values, and a "Declaration to the Deaf Church"—the result of a "think-tank" on this topic—is presented and expanded upon by Dr. Bob Ayres, author of *Deaf Diaspora: The Third Wave of Deaf Ministry* and founder of Deaf Teen Quest with essential insights from Dr. Rick McClain, a nationally renowned Deaf scholar, pastor, and educator. We invite you to join us in considering this challenge: How shall Deaf Churches and Ministries best move forward in the context of a highly secularized society?

Learn more at www.bobayres.com

What others are saying about
DEAFCHURCH 21: Vision for a New Generation

Jesus used "sign" language to reach people who were deaf to the gospel. He changed water to wine, fed the multitudes, and raised the dead to life. In *DEAFCHURCH 21,* Drs. Ayres and McClain explore the meaning of "signing" the gospel in the secular age. We hear first from those whose passion is to love the Deaf community with the good news of Jesus Christ. We are given a seat at the table for a lively discussion on the issues facing an effective and faithful ministry to the Deaf world. The authors face the challenges with honesty and hope, and develop a dynamic theology of ministry that takes the example of Jesus and the early church seriously. When Jesus said, "Whoever has ears, let them hear," he wasn't talking about sound waves; he was talking about the gospel. *DEAFCHURCH 21* is a clarion call to wisdom and to action.

Dr. Doug Webster
Professor, Beeson Divinity School, Samford University

Have you ever been pulled into a social media conversational thread because…well, you couldn't resist? That's the sense I had as I began reading *DEAFCHURCH 21*. The authenticity of the dialogue reminded me of how attracted I am to people who 'keep it real' – and how certain I am that faithful pointing to Jesus Christ in a world gone wacky may have more to do with our posture than our proclamations. Deaf believers are legitimately a distinct culture. This book's discussion is a gift from marginalized brothers and sisters in Christ that can encourage us all.

Dr. Dave Rahn
Sr. Ministry Advisor, Youth For Christ USA

DEAFCHURCH 21: Vision for a New Generation explores both the *Missio* and *Communio* components of ministry with, for and by persons who are Deaf. Embracing the contemporary challenges of our intensely secularized society, the authors have provided a resource for current and future pastoral workers in Deaf ministry to explore and reflect on how to best support Deaf persons through their spiritual faith journeys, both in our own faith traditions and collaboratively from an interfaith perspective. A "must read" for those called to leadership in the Deaf Church. An inspiring invitation to encounter and accompany!

Mary O'Meara, Executive Director
Department of Special Needs Ministry,
Archdiocese of Washington, DC

Drs. Ayres and McClain have written a must-read primer for anyone considering the Deaf Ministry. As a Deaf educator who teaches ASL and Deaf Culture at the University level and has been part of the Deaf ministries in different denominations, I agree that 'the sacred assembly across the ages has been one of helping to recognize, and even helping to usher in, the Kingdom of God.' And see this quote as a metaphor of how it's necessary for Deaf ministry to come together to partake in a spiritual quest to find God. I recommend this book to anyone who wants to educate themselves on Deaf ministry priorities and challenges.

Stephen J. Hardy, II,
ASL Lecturer at the University of Florida

The most successful Deaf Churches/Ministries, for decades, have been generational churches, often not affecting the generation prior nor just after their own. Historically, as congregational members age and die—so does the work. *DEAFCHURCH 21: Vision for a New*

Generation both academically and spiritually recognizes, addresses, and challenges these well-worn trends. The text is a clarion call for young Deaf men and women who are born again and led by the Spirit to respond to the Spirit's wooing to reach beyond generational margins into the Deaf Community with the purity of Christ's message of hope and healing. This is definitely a good read for all and worthy of use in academic settings.

Dr. JoAnn L. Smith,
Director, University of Valley Forge Deaf Ministry Program

Much like a trip to my local optometrist, *DEAFCHURCH 21* thoughtfully and boldly adjusted the lens of my soul to see with clarity the issues and opportunities that face the Deaf and Hard of Hearing communities across our country. I felt a deepening conviction, even as the power of the transformational message of Christ was amplified. This is a call to action: One that the church of Jesus Christ must honor. While the lens of my soul is now calibrated to see the problem in a fresh way, so is the clarity of hope that comes when followers of Jesus live into their calling.

Dan Wolgemuth
President/CEO, Youth For Christ USA

Grounded in strong scriptural understanding and sound theological doctrine (both provide a firm foundation for ministry) and infused with real-life examples directly from online and face-to-face focus groups, *DEAFCHURCH 21: Vision for a New Generation* presents a blueprint for successful Deaf ministry. Ayres and McClain tell this story as only people experienced in cultural understanding and grounded in authentic faith can tell.

Ben A. Sharpton
novelist, educator, minister

Having been part of a variety of Deaf ministries and churches for roughly 30 years, I have witnessed the birth of some, joined some in the middle of their growth, and sadly, seen others end. This book resonated with my experiences of what works and what doesn't. What Bob and Rick present here comes from sound wisdom and the Holy Spirit's guidance. The authors have reflected well our Lord's desire for Deaf people of all backgrounds to come and know Him. This book is an excellent tool to spur deep reflection if you desire to form a Deaf Church in this century.

Harry Wood
Teacher, Trainer, Youth Leader

Unlike historic efforts in this area, the authors draw on Deaf voices, as well as experienced Deaf and hearing church leaders, to identify historic failures of such ministries. Courageously, the authors address historic issues of oppression, empowerment, and the need to embrace the marginalized. Their challenge is rooted firmly in Biblical truths for achieving God's vision for *Deaf Ekklesia*. This text is an inspired "Vision for a new Generation"—must reading for anyone currently involved in Deaf ministry or thinking of setting up an outreach to members of the Deaf community.

Dr. Jan Humphrey
Educator, Ministry Leader, Certified Interpreter-Canada & US
Author of *So You Want to Be an Interpreter*

If you are looking for a prescriptive model for what a Deaf church should look like, you won't find it here. What you will find are thought provoking discussions to stimulate further thought about the unique challenges and opportunities of Deaf churches. One sentence in the book sums it up: 'The calling for the Deaf church is twofold: renewal of a faithful, biblical understanding of what it means to be the church in general and a specific commitment of the distinctiveness of a linguistic and cultural ministry to the Deaf community.

Terri Chapman, Director
SIL International Global Sign Languages Team

Whether you are in the ministry, an educator working with the Deaf, or are a Church historian, *DEAFCHURCH 21* offers readers a unique perspective on the historical contributions of the Church that have almost been forgotten. The book superbly succeeds in highlighting the Church's role in shaping today's Deaf culture, their understanding of spirituality, and identity within society. By means of social media, the authors capture the current challenges Deaf individuals in the Deaf Church community face on a daily basis. Furthermore, the book's structure allows for further thought and discussion at the end of each section and serves well as a course textbook.

Sharon M. DiFino, PhD, CCC-SLP
Clinical Assistant Professor, Speech, Language, and Hearing Sciences, UF

Students have touted *Deaf Diaspora: The Third Wave of Deaf Ministry* as one of the most influential books of their college studies. It is therefore thrilling to anticipate the effect this book will have on those in current and future ministry with Deaf people. It is a thorough and essential call to all who are involved with Deaf outreach, to keep the gospel of Christ central. The principles and values apply to both Deaf and Hearing Christians, and the collaborative effort to create a framework for application is a glorious glimpse of the Church carrying out Christ's mission.

Alta Johnson, Adjunct Professor,
ASL and Deaf Culture, Moody Bible Institute

DEDICATIONS AND ACKNOWLEDGMENTS
Dr. Rick McClain

To my wife of more than four decades, Deb

how she manages to keep me going when the embers of my passion run low… the breath of fresh air that reignites the flames of desire for education unto completion,

for my children, and my grandchildren. May this book be part of the legacy I am leaving with you; I pray that you'll be encouraged and inspired to be your best in service to our King and Savior, Jesus Christ.

"No man is an island unto himself," as John Donne wrote. No man ever accomplishes anything on his own efforts and abilities. I happily dedicate these efforts to several people. First, to my parents who have preceded me into their heavenly reward. They instilled within me a desire to excel, and to continue to grow. I wish they were alive today to see the fruit of their efforts and labor. To my sisters, Carol and Kathy; the earlier years brought much tribulation and difficulty. Living with me as the only son, and a Deaf one, could not have been easy. Their willingness to love and nurture me through the years has more than helped me become who I am today.

To all of my colleagues, friends and supporters: I have many to list, from the Seminary, to the Family Therapy community, to the faculty and staff at Beeson Divinity School, I give you my deepest appreciation for your encouragement and support. To Dr. Sharon and

Rev. Ray Berry, who allowed me the resources and means to complete my doctorate. To the many people that were a part of my reading committee, their suggestions and editing skills were immeasurable. To my friends and colleagues at Deaf Teen Quest, Deaf Online University, Tri-State Deaf School of Theology, and to the staff at Deaf Missions – all of whom allowed me every opportunity to practice and constantly work to perfect the theories and perceptions we are dealing with today.

I am not an island. I am not finished, for I am constantly becoming, simply through the encouragement I receive from all of you. To God be the Glory, great things He has done, is doing, and continues to do in the future!

DEDICATIONS AND ACKNOWLEDGMENTS

Dr. Bob Ayres

To my amazing wife, Kathryn Ayres, who walks alongside me in all of life's ventures,

as we strive to faithfully serve the Lord together, including in co-founding together an amazing ministry for Deaf and Hard of Hearing teenagers

to my children and grandchildren for bringing us such delight and adventure

and to my colleagues and friends in Deaf Teen Quest,

and throughout Youth for Christ USA

who inspire and encourage me in so many ways.

All praise and honor are lifted up to our resurrected Lord Jesus Christ for revealing the fullness of our Triune God through his perfect life and atoning sacrifice. Through His grace and mercy, God brought Kathryn Casey Ayres into my life as friend, companion, advisor, and comforter in this journey of marriage we've shared for over four decades. This adventure includes wonderful children, Christina, David, Casey, John, Ana, and Robert (who is like a son), amazing grandchildren, and a wealth of great friendships.

There have been many key mentors and influences in my life including my siblings: Bert, Alan, and Joy. I wrote *Real-Life Wisdom* to tell about several of these influencers. My "cloud of witnesses" on earth is joined by others in heaven, including my father and mother, Boyd and Ruth, who taught me to value lifelong education as an expression of the abundant life. It is a privilege to have studied under many outstanding professors at Beeson Divinity School of Samford University. I am thankful in particular for Drs. Douglas Webster and Mark Searby who helped integrate my doctoral education into a practical framework. The insights provided related to my dissertation (upon which this book is based) by Mary O'Meara, Robert Rhoads, Mark Seeger, and Jack Miller are invaluable. I am grateful to Jennifer Milton-Houlton for her expertise and excellence in feedback and editing.

Last but not least, I am deeply indebted to those who served with Dr. McClain and me as part of the "think-tank" on this vital topic: Matthew Belwood, Noah Buchholz, Mary Beth Cantrell, Joe Dixon, Chad Entinger, Michael Gonzalez, Lamonte Grant, Stephen Hause, Todd Miller, Bruce Persons, and Marvella Sellers. I appreciate greatly Jessica Belwood, Dallas and Emily Brock, Kathy Ayres and my son David for working behind the scenes to make the praxis possible. These relationships affirm the African proverb, "If you want to go fast, go alone; if you want to go far, go with others."

TABLE OF CONTENTS

Foreword

Chad Entinger, CEO
Deaf Missions, Council Bluffs, IA

Deaf people remain among the least reached people groups in the United States and around the world today. This statement alone justifies the need and significance for this book. Too many Deaf people do not know Jesus as their Lord and personal Savior. Deaf churches are dwindling and many are closing. It's getting harder and harder in an increasingly secular world to reach lost Deaf people.

Compounding the problem is the lack of available resources that clearly and effectively communicate the Gospel of Jesus with Deaf people, particularly those with appeal to a younger, more secular audience. Current real-life challenges are rarely addressed in resources, especially with thoughtful solutions provided by Deaf people and those who serve alongside Deaf people in ministry.

I could not be more honored and privileged to write this Foreword for *DEAFCHURCH 21: Vision for a New Generation* by Dr. Bob Ayres and Dr. Rick McClain. Bob and Rick are long-time dear friends and colleagues in Deaf ministry. Together they write and teach with a combined depth of wisdom and knowledge from having served in Deaf ministry for several decades. I've been blessed to participate in the numerous training sessions, lectures and sermons given by them throughout the years. They are the wisest of the sages who have enlightened me (and countless others) deeply, and been of tremendous encouragement to me spiritually, personally and professionally. I am honored to serve Jesus with them.

Dr. Ayres and Dr. McClain humbly sought out and gathered insights through think-tank sessions with fellow colleagues and professionals representing a variety of backgrounds and experiences within the Deaf ministry world. What a joy it was for me to be among those participating in those sessions. I wholeheartedly believe they will inspire and instruct you through this book and the process they went through in developing these insights.

Two years of social media discussions on the topic of the "21st Century Deaf Church," and the conclusions and interpretations from the think-tank sessions resulting in fourteen points of the "Declaration to the Deaf Church" with insights and explanations – combined with theological and biblical foundations – provide valuable foundations and frameworks from which viable and impactful ministries can be developed and built.

This book is a benchmark for the future of the Deaf church. The vision presented here is compelling. Best practices are clearly outlined and explained. At last, we really do have a path forward and upward. *DEAFCHURCH 21* provides the insights, but we have to do the hard work of leading Deaf churches and ministries into the future, faithfully and with excellence.

Now is the time for the Deaf church to rise up and rely on the Holy Spirit's power to free Deaf people from oppression, exclusion, isolation and marginalization. It's time for us all to genuinely unite and work together to overcome challenges and barriers in reaching Deaf people with the hope found in knowing Jesus. It's time to press onward with the expectation that many, many Deaf people will be among those with us in heaven "*...from every nation, tribe, people and language, standing before the throne and before the Lamb.*" (Revelation 7:9 NIV).

It's time! Let's go!

Discovery and Hope

Welcome to this journey of discovery and hope for the future of the Deaf Church! Let's start with the bad news… what is generally being done in our local churches currently is not sustainable, or even appropriate for younger generations. They are raised in a world dramatically different from previous age groups. There is little cause to describe this new reality but there is plenty of reason to prayerfully adapt. Now, here is the good news: none of these dramatic changes as a result of the secularization of our culture comes as a surprise to God! "Jesus Christ is the same yesterday and today and forever" (Hebrews 13:8). However, these rapid changes in our world demand we embrace new ways of thinking when it comes to evangelism, formation, discipleship, and service. The gospel remains eternal but the post-modern context focuses us to thoughtful conversations and intentional decisions about church priorities, values, practices, and structure. To experience renewal in the Deaf Church, willingness to address difficult questions is necessary for plotting a reasonable plan of action. Our efforts are to position ourselves faithfully in response to what the Holy Spirit is doing. Change always involves taking risks and often requires embracing new paradigms of life as part of a missional community of reconciliation. God can lead us to fruitful ministry within a secular culture without abandoning our historic faith and biblical theology.

The journey that led to this book began in September 2012 with the establishment of a Facebook group called "21st Century Deaf Church". This discussion group on Facebook began with fifty-five personal contacts. During the two years the Facebook group remained open, more than 200 people were added by their own request or recommendation by others in the group. Considering the limited number of people involved in Deaf ministry, this group would be considered sizable and members representative of many churches, denominations, and Deaf ministries. Most in the group maintained a high level of thoughtful interactions and comments. The growth and participation in this group discussion helped confirm the assumption of the need for a new vision of Deaf Church for the next generations.

With help from friend and colleague, Dr. Rick McClain, a diverse group of Deaf[1] ministry leaders were brought together by Bob Ayres to serve as a "Think-Tank" for determining *essential priorities* for ministry with the next generation of young adults. As the founder and director of Deaf Teen Quest, Dr. Ayres was often confronted by the challenges of connecting young people, who aged-out of the high school ministry, with local churches. Likewise, it is difficult for Deaf young adults to find Deaf Churches or Deaf Ministries in churches that meet their spiritual, relational, and emotional needs. This journey emerged from a deep concern about the lack of youth and young adult sensitive fellowships and the overall survival of current and future Deaf churches.

In a departure from the structure of most academic books, *DEAFCHURCH 21* begins with the informal and moves towards the

1 Capital "D" in Deaf is used when referring to the people group and is usually followed by a noun: community, culture, church, etc. This reflects a widely accepted view on the cultural aspects of this identifiable population. Lower-case "d" is used when specifically identifying an individual or the physical trait of deafness.

more academic. The reason for this unusual structure is to allow for both the casual reader who will respond to the narrative style as well as the classroom student who will pursue a deeper contemplation of the process and theological and biblical foundations. Therefore, there are several shifts between first-person to third-person narrative between certain sections. Wherever practical, this is smoothed out for readability.

DEAFCHURCH 21: Vision for a New Generation is designed to create space for the Holy Spirit to work in your heart and ministry by asking the hard questions and encouraging you to act upon the answers you discern. This book is designed to be read as an individual, studied in a classroom or small group, or used by church or ministry leadership for strategic planning. Whether you are reading this as an individual seeking ideas for establishing a faith community, a Pastor or church leader in search of a meaningful model for church, a study group thinking strategically, or a student using this as a textbook, our hope is to broaden the possibilities for the emergence—by the power of the Holy Spirit—of a vibrant faith community that offers wholeness and purpose for those in the Deaf Community. Our prayer is DEAFCHURCH 21 will provide a legitimate framework in creating vision for reaching future generations in your ministry context.

Finally, an important disclaimer: the opinions and perspectives of the authors, both individually or collectively, do not necessarily reflect the individual views of participants in the think-tank, other than to have found consensus on the challenges facing today's Deaf Church and producing a two-part *Declaration*. The authors expand upon this declaration with a *Call* to Deaf Churches and Ministries. Perspectives of the participants vary, and may or may not agree with the written conclusions of Drs. Ayres and McClain. Although the participants provided essential insights as part of the research for this book, all conclusions and other written content not otherwise referenced are exclusively the work of Drs. Ayres and McClain. Opinions and statements by participants are carefully identified with proper credit given. Ayres & McClain Publishing is committed to creating platforms for Christian scholarship in the Deaf Community, particularly within younger generations to be encouraged, elevated, and recognized.

Once again, welcome to this journey of discovery. We invite you to engage in this book as though you are part of this think-tank; because in some ways you are included through reading this material. Now is the time to try a different approach, to take more responsibility, and even bold risks. We pray that God use *DEAFCHURCH 21: Vision for a New Generation* to create space for the Holy Spirit to move visibly in your life as you intentionally consider how you are called to respond. We serve an amazing God, who calls us to abide and follow. The best is yet to come!

Dr. Bob Ayres

Dr. Rick McClain

All scriptural references are in English Standard Version (ESV) unless otherwise noted.

Background Information

Reliable statistics are difficult to come by but an acceptable estimate of the birthrate of children with discernable hearing loss is 1.7 per 1,000 births with an increase to 2-3 per 1000 within the first few years of life.[2] What may be startling to those unfamiliar with the Deaf community are the vast numbers of deaf children in today's world raised without sign language in the home. For every ten children born with hearing loss, only one is born to parents who are also deaf. Deaf children, who are born to parents who are deaf, develop socially and cognitively at similar rates as hearing children born to hearing parents; both enjoy the benefits of language-rich environments from birth. One child (of the ten born deaf) has hearing parents who reach some level of sign language fluency. The remaining eight of these ten children are born in hearing families who never learn fluency in sign language. As one might imagine, these communication barriers create a myriad of challenges. Acquisition of language is universally understood as vital for cognitive and social development yet there are varying perspectives on the importance of lip-reading and speech. Those with a cultural perspective maintain that deafness should not be considered a disability and communication barriers are created by the lack of signing. We agree but expand this view to include whatever works to bridge

---

2 2016 CDC's Hearing Screening and Follow-up Survey, cdc.gov/ncbddd/hearingloss/data.html, and National Institutes of Health, "Quick Statistics About Hearing", nidcd.nih.gov/health/statistics/quick-statistics-hearing#1, both accessed May 3, 2019.

the communication gaps. Technology helps but human connections are vital. Helen Keller is quoted, "Blindness separates me from things; deafness separates me from people."[3]

In spite of setbacks brought about by the infamous Milan Conference in 1880[4] regarding education of the deaf—banning use of sign language in Deaf education in Western Europe and the United States—by the twentieth century, the linguistic-cultural survival of the Deaf Community was evident primarily in residential schools, social clubs, and Deaf churches. Much of the effectiveness of Deaf Churches was connected to a widely established Christian[5] society and value system of the past, with religious instruction common in public schools, including the residential Schools for the Deaf. In fact, many of the residential schools were begun by Christian ministers, parents, and educators.[6] Chaplains, guest pastors, and Bible classes were commonplace. Until late in the twentieth century, the majority of Deaf children attended residential schools—returning home only for summers and Christmas holidays—and nearby churches of various denominations established religious instruction both on and off the campus. Teaching from the Bible was viewed as part of a well-rounded formal education. Deaf students also had many examples of culturally

---

3 Barbara Silverstone, *The Lighthouse Handbook On Vision Impairment and Vision Rehabilitation*. Vol. 1 (Oxford: Oxford University Press, 2000), 469.

4 The Council of Milan was an international meeting of educators for deaf children on September 6-11, 1880 in Italy where eight resolutions were presented against any use of sign language in Deaf education. By a vote of 160 to 4, delegates passed "oral-only" resolutions which resulted in widespread negative ramifications for deaf and hard of hearing individuals both educationally and socially.w

5 The term "Christian" is used here and throughout the book as a descriptor of the entire spectrum of the religious groups that would identify as part of the historic Judeo-Christian tradition.

6 For the best resource to learn about the role of the church in the founding of Deaf schools in America, check out *Deaf Heritage: A Narrative History of Deaf America* by Jack Gannon.

Deaf Christian adult role models among the residential school administrators, educators, and staff.

In 1975, Congress passed the Education of All Handicapped Children Act (Public Law 94–142) which ultimately resulted in *educational mainstreaming* as one means of fulfilling the mandate to provide all children with a "free appropriate public education in the least restrictive environment and with accommodations."[7] Nothing has been more impactful on the effectiveness of the Deaf Church than changes in the educational system.[8] By the 1990s, approximately 80% of Deaf/HH students were mainstreamed into public schools in their communities as a result of these changes. For the most part, even those attending residential schools began returning home for weekends and missing out on vibrant Deaf Communities and related activities in connection with the residential schools. There are many positive aspects of educational mainstreaming—including deaf children being able to live at home with their families—however, the negative results include a dramatic rise in isolation of scattered deaf students. This shift threatened the existence of Deaf culture and ASL through the lack of healthy socialization with peers and positive role models.

---

7 Bob Ayres, *Deaf Diaspora: The Third Wave of Deaf Ministry* (Lincoln, NE: iUniverse, 2004). In this book, I further expand on the unintended social and spiritual ramifications of the Education of All Handicapped Children Act (P.L. 94–142 and P.L. 99–457) replaced in 1990 by IDEA–Individuals with Disabilities Education Act (P.L. 105–17); these changes in the educational system ultimately brought about a dispersing of the Deaf community, 20-25.

8 For those interested in deeper study of the educational research, we recommend resources such as "Journal of Deaf Studies and Deaf Education" (https://academic.oup.com/jdsde), "Journal of American Sign Language and Literatures" (http://journalofasl.com/), and resources available at Gallaudet University (https://www.gallaudet.edu/library/research).

As a result of the 1963–1969 rubella measles epidemic that impacted pregnant women[9], a dramatic increase occurred in the number of deaf and blind children born during those years. As the population boomed (as many as three or four times previous levels) and they became youth and young adults, there arose a widespread discontent (similar to other "rights" movements led by youthful populations) with a strong "anti-hearing" bias based on perceived and real oppression. The pinnacle of this era was the 1988 *Deaf President Now!* protests at Gallaudet University. Since 1864, when authorization was given by Congress to confer college degrees, the trustees had never selected a Deaf president. This student-led movement was an exemplar of effective public protest, and led to the replacement of a newly-selected hearing president by I. King Jordan, the first Deaf president of the University. *Deaf President Now!* is a defining moment for current Deaf cultural identity and collective empowerment.

Within the Deaf Community, there remains a deeply-held resentment for a long legacy of oppression. For many, the Christian faith becomes a focal-point of resentment because of the view that "religious people try to control my body with their morality". The net result was the Christian faith in the Deaf community teetered on the brink of extinction by the final decade of the twentieth century as it struggled to exist in an almost completely secularized Deaf Community. Those leading Deaf Churches and ministries labored in an almost completely secularized Deaf culture.[10] Identifying this spiritual crisis is not the end of the story, but does provide a good starting place for beginning to address the many current and future challenges in the Deaf Church.

---

9 "Rubella", The History of Vaccines: an educational resource by the College of Physicians of Philadelphia, accessed May 26, 2015, http://www.historyofvaccines.org/content/articles/rubella.

10 Ayres, *Deaf Diaspora*, 34.

Timeline

1964-1969	Rubella Measles outbreak in US (increase in number of deaf children)
1964	*Dictionary of American Sign Language on Linguistic Principles*[11]
1973	Vocational Rehab Act/Section 504 (disabilities civil rights legislation)
1975	ADA and IDEA acts for (educational and vocational access)
1988	*Deaf President Now!* Gallaudet (recognition of Deaf empowerment)
1990s	Technology expansion (communication and information)
1990-2000s	Educational Mainstreaming (shift from residential schools; scattering)
2010-2020s	Deafhood—Children of DPN generation (capable and empowered)

11 William Stokoe, Dorothy C. Casterline, Carl Croneberg. Based on linguistic research that became the foundation for acceptance of American Sign Language as a legitimate language with its own grammar, syntax, and linguistic morphology.

CHAPTER I—Clarifying Issues

Facebook Discussion Threads

This opening section begins with excerpts of comments posted in an online Facebook discussion group: 21st Century Deaf Church (21cDC). All comments in this chapter are used with permission. The excerpts are rearranged by topic and edited for clarity and space. This structure may give the appearance of a closed conversation among a small group of people, but this is not the case. The opinions are of these individuals do not necessarily reflect their current views or perspectives of others in the group, including the authors. The interactions of this discussion group allowed for ideas to form, develop, and sometimes change. Consider these comments as you might a conversation with friends. Often people are writing as they processed their thoughts. Dialogue is a valuable narrative form of how ideas can emerge through respectful discourse. This conversation provides a doorway into the journey of exploring meaningful models of church, particularly from those who are part of the Deaf community.

Though their contributions are not included in the text, I particularly want to thank Gary and Rhonda Barnett, Jacob Buchholz, Mary Beth Cantrell, Chad Entinger, Robbie Godbold, Marshall Lawrence, Kinna Smith, Mike Olson, Denise Pulfer, Mark Seeger, Jeremey Stockman, William Timmers, Billy Widener, and Blake Widmer among many others for their uniquely thoughtful participation in the overall discussion.

21st Century Deaf Church (21cDC)

Online Discussion Group

Introductory Comments for the Facebook Group

"What is the nature of the Deaf Church of the 21st Century? It seems clear that it will function differently than earlier years. We live in a highly secularized society. This group is a place to discuss these questions. Even if you already are part of a Deaf Church, we are compelled by Christ to 'look down the road' and strive to be faithful in staying true to the Gospel yet adapting to the changing culture in today's world.

I suspect many are pondering these same things that I am... how do we respond to the needs of next generations of Christian deaf and hard of hearing young adults? Do we continue to have old discussions about Deaf Church vs. Deaf ministry in a hearing church or ask ourselves the hard questions that face us now... are we on the right path into the future for ministry with this next generation, particularly youth and young adults?

One thing I am convinced of... we cannot continue to do the same thing and expect a different result. We must enter this topic full of prayer and humility that God is doing a new thing. I have my own opinions but they have not become entrenched positions. I am hopeful to share with and learn from each of you." – Bob Ayres

Being the Church

Bob Ayres

Here is something to chew upon... "Church" is not something we "go to"; it is something we ARE... the Body of Christ. Therefore, we have to rediscover what it means to BE CHURCH in our current cultural context.

The Gospel "that was once for all delivered to the saints" (Jude 3) is unchanging; we do not have permission to change the scriptural truths passed down for 4000+ years. However, to keep these truths authentic (including life found only in Jesus Christ), we are compelled to study the culture in which we live and remove barriers for applying truth to secular society. I believe the 21st Century Deaf Church will have a much more outward focus at its center than 20th Century Deaf Church. Christian maturity exhibits itself when it is no longer what God can do FOR me... but what God can do THROUGH me for others. My pastor uses the descriptive phrases about who we are as a church: "Becoming like Jesus for the sake of others." and "Becoming an extending family on mission." Mission takes on a much broader, more practical identity than "missions" or "evangelism"; it becomes about being a Body of Christ focused on living out that faith as doers of the word (James). How does this resonate with you?

Jessica Belwood: I think with our present church, we accepted our roles of being a spectator when we sit in the pews to listen to a pastor. If we have to be activists, to be DOERS of the Word, we have to figure out how to empower the assembly/church/Body to go out. A few things on my heart. I think it's important we intentionally return to houses for churches. A house has its limits for a reason- when the church grows and reaches the limits of the size of a house, it's a tell-tale sign to plant a new church and to train up new leaders to lead the church so we don't get trapped in the megachurch mindset (no offense to anyone). People can become just "numbers", and we miss the opportunity to raise up great leaders.

Matthew Belwood: Something hit me recently from the blog of a former professor (adorate.org/2012/10/phony-baloney-in-church.html): "Psychiatrist M. Scott Peck once wryly observed that an AA meeting is more like the church than the church is like the church...", "... AA, on the other hand, demands each one joining must acknowledge terribly embarrassing personal failures. The challenging realization is to acknowledge, for much the same reason, AA forms a community, while church is more often simply a group...", "...Community is the product of people who are together, not by choice, but by the certainty that they cannot make it on their own. For these men and women, the community itself, as empowered by the Spirit of God, is a fundamental and essential part of their own redemption. Like people walking into an AA meeting, the ticket into a genuine community is not the pretense of accomplishments but the admission of failures. No one can lead an AA meeting other than an alcoholic. And, in brutal speaking truth to self, everyone in that community knows that sobriety is never achieved, it is only maintained -- and often only barely maintained -- by everyone in the room. Everyone. They are led from the inside..."

Bruce Persons: Interesting you brought up how AA meetings are like a community and a church like a group and how some felt that AA meetings are better than church. Last month, I went to a couple of AA meetings for my Pastoral Counseling class and I would not trade anything for the experience I had. I met several active Christians who are recovering alcoholics and they consider it an extension of their church and even their own unique ministry. All of them admitted that they could not come around to confessing to their fellow brothers and sisters in Christ due to fears of shame, judgment, and rejection, if not only their own pastor. I think that the principle of confession, transparency, and authentic living with one another in the context of a community is something that must be chewed upon and integrated into the fabric of church life. The challenge is the ever-present question of "how?"

Noah Buchholz: "Pastor, not friend" | The Christian Century | (christiancentury.org/article/2012-12/pastor-not-friend)

I've discussed this topic with one of my pastoral mentors. He pointed out that Jesus told his disciples that they are his friends now (John 15:15). He also said, "All the coolest people in the town go to my church. Whom am I supposed to be friends with if I can't be their friends?" While he was partly kidding, he was saying something that can be very true for Deaf ministers. He is a pastor of a hearing church in a large suburban community in New York City area, so it is still possible for him to befriend some good people outside his church. Nevertheless, it is a completely different situation for Deaf ministers. It's hard to find a good Deaf Christian in the area that doesn't attend your church. If you find one, then you would ask... why doesn't this person go to my church? (It is rare to find more than one or two Deaf churches in the 30-mile radius.) If you are told that you should befriend other Deaf pastors only, you know that would not be enough, because Deaf pastors are spread all over the country. There are also many other issues at stake regarding this topic. What are your thoughts about what this article has to say? Make sure to read comments below the article.

Jessica Belwood: I wonder if it's a good idea to reserve a full day for church with a focus on three aspects- abiding, fellowship/worship, and going out to serve. My husband and I consider Sunday a "work day" (while reserving another day of the week to be our Sabbath). We drive around and pick up teenagers and go to a church service, then hang out in the afternoon. I wonder if the future church will benefit from intentionally returning to homes, carving out time during the "service/meeting/fellowship/worship" for each member to abide in Christ, share His Word with each other and then GO OUT and serve somewhere weekly (homeless shelter, soup kitchen, nursing homes, etc.). Another reason why it may be beneficial to return to houses is that women can be more involved (especially mothers with young kids!).

Bob Ayres: The other reality is that the church is where "the incredibly vulnerable and the terribly contagious" interact. Care must be given to creating healing communities and not germ factories. It is essential for pastors to surround themselves with trusted friends who are wise, dependable and can keep confidence. Always keep the lights on in friendships. Having confidentiality is different from having secrets. We can only get better when we are honest with ourselves and others. Transparency, therefore, is where we are "wise as serpents and gentle as doves." You are transparent with others at the appropriate levels that they can handle, that you can trust them and that glorifies God. You need trusted, quality friends wherever you can find them. Some need to be local. The key is how transparent you are with each of them. Every Christian definitely needs at least two or three with whom they can be totally transparent with and know that they will still love you at your most vulnerable.

Matthew Belwood: I continue to remind myself that the future doesn't have to be what I consider "comfortable" relative to my experience. I love ASL and the way things have been and encourage preservation efforts. I also recognize that the future may mean something different, something new. Might have a lot of people with cochlear implants. Might be more English. Might not be what we have experienced. It's not a sin for culture to evolve, as long as culture is not breaking God's commandments. We don't worship Deaf culture and ASL. Maybe God is allowing changes because if we "worship" these things too much, they become idols. So...It will be a new day. A new wine. A new wine skin. I ask God to give me the right attitude and flexibility to reach others despite the changes we might face in the future of possible changes in the communication preferences of deaf people. I take greater comfort that Jesus is the same today, yesterday, and tomorrow.

Rick McClain: Two things to remember: 1) God's love is always stronger than anything we will ever be up against. The Love of God never leaves us without an avenue to best reach the deaf. Certainly, in the 1960's there was a certain "process" and a definite journey in maturity to reach the next generation. We are now in an introspective period where we must come before the Lord to inquire of His heart, His desire, and His will. What does Jesus want? It cannot ever be what the deaf culture wants, for we can see the acculturalization of the gospel weakens the impact, message and hope of the gospel.

2) We must remember, there will always be deaf people. Technology may change the approach of deafness, but it will never remove deafness - either as a culture, or as a medical reality. Here is something to consider: God made the deaf and blind as a means to an expression of His glory in their changed lives. Isaiah 29 reminds us

that the deaf will hear the words of this book. The blinded eyes will be opened. We will, indeed, see the Salvation of our Lord.

Matthew Belwood: Art and Worship in the 21st Century Deaf Church – this is something I have been pondering for a long while. We need more art, poetry, and aesthetics to govern our videos. Architecture and colors of the places we meet. Complex because we cannot just copy hearing and worldly things and call it "deaf art and worship" (though that's what I find myself doing often). Why has art lost its importance in the church? How do we bring it back? How do we make our "music?" This article by Lecrae in the Huffington Post is very insightful- it raises so many themes of what it means to produce art and music, yes, but also how our separationist Christian culture keeps non-Christians out and weakens our art (and outreach). "This Is What Happens When Hip-Hop Lets The Saints In" by Jon Ward (m.huffpost.com/us/entry/4784064).

Bob Ayres: Deaf Poetry Jam/Slam – At a recent conference with DTQ staff, an urban poet gave an amazing series of "spoken word" poetry as is popular in some urban coffee shop settings. Would ASL Poetry be a good way to reach non-Christian Deaf young adults? Would this be a good way to bond, share the gospel as part of your story, and reach lost folks in environments where they feel most comfortable? Could Deaf Poetry come alongside Music and Drama as a part of worship? What are your thoughts?

ASL SLAM "offers the stage to audience members to come up and rap, rhapsodize and rehash or just to relate in sign language." (www.aslslam.com)

"Deaf Jam: American Sign Language Meets Slam Poetry " a film by Judy Lieff (pbs.org/independentlens/deaf-jam/film.html)[12]

Rick McClain: Three questions remain in my heart with this issue we are facing in this discussion. One, when Jesus said that "if anyone must follow me, he must deny himself, take up his cross and follow me," what did he mean? What is it that we love and cherish the most in our lives, today? ASL? Deaf Culture? What is our definition? What ignites our driving force? Oftentimes, we are guilty of replacing the eternal with the temporal. 1 John reminds us not to love the things of this world, and reminds us that the greatest thing we can do is to reconcile our Love and our belief together. Only then will we not only NOT be shaped by the culture, but we will be able to be a shaping force in our culture. Jesus did, and through the life changing experiences of his disciples, they turned the world upside down.

Discussion Questions

1. How might isolation become a threat to the leadership of a Deaf Church or Ministry? What are some ways that this challenge can be overcome in healthy ways?

2. What are the pros and cons of having a separate Deaf Church versus having a Deaf Ministry within the context of a larger church?

3. How might creative expressions of worship—art, dance, music, video, poetry—impact the Deaf Church positively? What might be the downside to these modalities?

---

12 Thanks to Mike Olson for leads to this information.

4. What points made in the discussion thread did you agree or disagree with? What questions were asked that you see as essential ones to consider?

Deeper Dive: Describe your paradigm of "church"? What does it mean to be a Christian in your tradition? How does the Deaf Church fit into your denominational structure?

Advocacy and Audism

Noah Buchholz

Deaf churches should be involved in the local and global Deaf communities not as a mere spectator but as an activist. The Bible teaches us to help those who are weak, oppressed, and poor. The Deaf are certainly a group of weak, oppressed, and poor. In fact, the Deaf are one of the most forgotten and oppressed cultural groups around the world. We must follow Jesus' example by reaching people not through only teaching but also serving and advocating. Nowadays, in the 21st century, the language and culture of Deaf people are being seriously threatened by the ever-growing power of audism. Deaf churches ought to step in and advocate for Deaf people, fighting against injustice to which Deaf people are enslaved. One way for Deaf churches to be involved in the Deaf community and advocate for Deaf people is celebrating the International Week of the Deaf. Celebrating the International Week of the Deaf is a way to preserve Deaf culture and language, and to educate hearing people about Deaf culture. Of course, there are many other ways to advocate for Deaf culture; thus, I encourage Deaf churches to be creative and come up with different ways to serve the Deaf community. Remember, as Martin Luther King Jr. says, "We must use time creatively, and forever realize that the time is always ripe to do right."

Bruce Persons: Great insight that you have presented here. In order to understand your vision better, I have several questions for you with respect to advocacy. First, what is your exact definition of advocacy (beyond "liberating the weak, oppressed, and poor") as God calls us to do in the Bible and beyond what Jesus did by speaking out against those who have oppressed the least in the society? Would you label "social justice" under your definition of advocacy?

Second, what is the core motive behind advocacy? What is the ultimate goal here that we are trying to achieve? Is it merely about freeing the victims of the society who have been wronged and bringing justice to the unjust world marred by sin, or is it about calling them out of darkness and sin into the light so that they may experience authentic transformation and live in the light of Jesus Christ's resurrection and victory over sin?

Noah Buchholz: Bruce, I didn't quite have an exact definition for "advocacy" in my mind. I was thinking about helping people, serving people, standing up for people, etc. Yeah, "social justice" is what I was thinking about. To answer your second question, I would say both. I don't want to help people just to draw them to Christ. I also want to help them because they are human beings like every one of us and feel pain like we do. Helping them also includes speaking against oppressors and calling for justice in this world, because we need to help oppressors to realize their wrongdoings. Jesus Christ told the group of sheep that they are being rewarded because they serve people, give people food and clothes, and visit people in jail, not because they have won a certain number of souls. Also, Jesus asks a rhetorical question, "If you have an ox that falls into a well on the Sabbath, wouldn't you take hold of it and lift it out?" We know that human beings are much more valuable than animals and human beings everywhere are suffering and being trapped in this dark world. Of course, I hope that people whom we serve see the light of Christ, not ours, through our compassion and deeds, and, as a result, realize that the only hope of true redemption we have is in Christ.

Bruce Persons: The reason why I asked you to define "advocacy" and whether it was linked to social justice is because our generation has embraced this "buzz word" almost as if it was a religion by itself. In an attempt to be more relevant to the post-modern generation, churches have embraced a secular definition of what justice is (that is, social justice) and assimilated it into the framework of congregational life at the expense of the Gospel message. Consequently, the Gospel message is watered down, Jesus is pushed to the sidelines, a Biblical view of justice gets distorted, and people believe that justice depends on humanity's efforts to right the wrong and free the oppressed (in other words, eradicate the sin on their own so that an Utopian society can be realized where everyone is happy).

Moreover, advocacy is not simply about bringing justice to this world (it will not happen until the Lord returns to judge everyone) but also about empowering (not merely helping/enabling) Deaf and Hard of Hearing people to abide in Christ and experience an abundant life with one another in the midst of our broken and sin-ridden life. While churches are expected to speak out against injustice, churches must never neglect to preach the gospel, calling people to be disciples of Christ by being faithful and obedient to his commandments, and ultimately become missional-minded. I found an excellent article on this topic: thechristianworldview.com/tcwblog/archives/741

Bob Ayres: My concern is that these topics such as Deaf Rights and Advocacy, regardless of how powerful and true, will become a fad that church-members rally around for only a short while. We wouldn't want it to be a "topic", but rather a lifestyle of living out Christ in a broken world. I wonder if we practice and teach these values by empowering deaf and hard of hearing folks to 1) abide in Christ 2) live in true community 3) be doers of the word then we draw them into a transformative, missional community.

Jessica Belwood: One thing I'm wondering is if we might be skipping a few too many ladder rungs to reach the social issue of audism? To me, the lowest and the most basic ladder rung in the social issues that impact Deaf people the most is the hierarchy of needs (Maslow), and the impact of the self-actualization of a person primarily comes from their family of origin. I've been looking around and meeting many awesome Deaf ministry leaders, but I've noticed that the majority of them come from a pretty healthy family. In the deaf school that Matt and I work in reaching the Deaf teens- probably 90% of the students' parents have separated, creating a fractured family. Very few have full access with communication with their own family. That leads to a downward spiral in where we can lose so many potential Deaf leaders to step up to the issue of audism. Healthy family begets healthy leaders. We might not be able to fight audism if we lose more children to destructive families. I wonder if we need to shift our focus of advocacy of the Deaf through their families. How can the church do that?

Rick McClain: Social Justice Holiness (as the Wesleyan-Arminians like to call it) has actually been considered as "advocacy" from the beginning of John Wesley's time. As one who formerly studied Church History, I am of the opinion that events of the Reformation were an issue of not only "social justice" advocacy, but also in "spiritual justice" advocacy.

A Christian who is not involved in the changing of the world is not a Christian in the active sense of the word. One cannot be deaf to the plights of the community and be considered "Christian." That, in itself, is simply mental assent to which I have understood Jesus would respond, "Depart from me you who practice evil! I never knew you."

The invariable attempts our world has made at cultural exaltation at the expense of a proper, God-Centered perspective in human dignity knows no limits, and yet do provide us with an opportunity to glorify God in the presence of men – an opportunity to serve a broken world, an opportunity to be light in a world of darkness, and an opportunity to provide a drink of water in Jesus' name.

Noah Buchholz: Jessica is right to say that we need to help Deaf children with their family situations. I observe that many Deaf children's family situations are not good because of language and cultural barriers. 1) Some hearing parents don't know how to sign and they can't communicate with their Deaf children. I don't need to explain more how this causes bad family life. 2) Some hearing parents feel at loss with how to raise Deaf children. As a result, they neglect their Deaf children or feel overwhelmed. 3) Deaf parents of Deaf children probably come from a hearing family who did not raise them well because of cultural and language barriers. As a result, Deaf parents don't discipline Deaf children well. 4) Some Deaf children live in dorms and dorm parents are not able to discipline them in the way parents are able to. Also, they never truly experience family life. 5) Some Deaf parents grew up in dorms where they never learned about good family life. As a result, they do not know how to foster a good family life. I can keep going but I will end here for now. My point is that most Deaf children's family situations are linked to audism. If we help to eliminate audism, we will be able to help many Deaf children with their family situations.

Rick McClain: One of the reasons Christianity has been able to withstand the changes of time through the various labels that have been attributed to it is because it is not a metatheory (while our atheists friends might disagree, here), but a complex system that has a complete, well-constructed, defensible, and perpetual philosophical base that resolves philosophical issues and dilemma.

Noah Buchholz: (myfoxphoenix.com/story/23751124/2013/10/21/tempe-apartments-for-the-deaf-accused-of-discrimination) We, Deaf ministry leaders, need to wake up and take notice of discriminations against our people around us. If we are to bring God's light to the Deaf community, we must stand up for those who are weak and oppressed. I respect those who believe that we should not focus on this kind of thing because we need to focus on the "afterlife" that God promises to us. BUT... please don't be either the Priest or Levite in the Good Samaritan parable. If you see someone is struggling or crying for help, don't just tell this person that Jesus loves her. Bandage her wounds, put her on your donkey, and bring her to a safe place where she will get help. That is LOVE, my friends, and it is what conquers evil. I pray that Deaf ministry leaders advocate for Deaf people in their local communities more. That is how we emulate Jesus Christ. Is anyone in this group from Phoenix? Know someone from there? I hope Deaf ministers there will do something about this.

Bob Ayres: How do we get past simply educating people about the issues of oppression, expressing outrage, and actually work as agents of change? It seems the secular world takes the lead and then Christians of good faith join in. Is there more? Certainly. One of the best examples (hearing or Deaf) of an effective social movement was the first *Deaf President Now!* protests. Not only was there a demonstration but the leadership presented a crystal-clear list of demands.

Oppression of anyone is oppression of all. We are freeing both the oppressed and the oppressor through simple acts of service and sometimes through civil disobedience. This does not mean neglecting our own for hundreds of other issues; it is intended to help mature our church memberships through looking at oppression of the Deaf in the context of the larger picture of oppression. Is this part of the practical application for this issue?

Discussion Questions

1. How would you describe "social justice" in the context of the Christian faith? What are some practical examples of serving the "weak, oppressed, and poor"?

2. Should the church be involved in protests, marches, and advocacy against injustice? If so, is that officially taking a position as a church or encouraging members to advocate?

3. What are the larger societal issues that also affect the Deaf Community that should be addressed? How should Deaf Churches participate in broader societal concerns?

Deeper Dive: If you were a pastor or influential leader in a Deaf Church or ministry, what scriptures would you point to as evidence of advocacy on behalf of those who are weak, oppressed, and poor? What do you see as the most prevailing social issues today? How do you balance the role of a peacemaker with the responsibility to actively resist injustice?

Theology and Creeds

Bruce Persons

Is our anemic growth and lack of interest in churches due to an addiction to entertainment and technology? Is it absolutely essential that we draw people into churches by resorting to the post-modern form of worship that depends on various subjective elements such as feelings, emotions, visual animations, etc., or is there some way for us to practice a simpler form of worship that, while incorporating a minimal amount of loud music and light effects, still draws people's attention to God's majesty and holiness and our deep need for a Savior? If you believe that we must depend on the subjective elements, how can we ensure that we remain faithful to the Scriptural mandate of Christ-centered preaching, God-honoring worship, relationally-healthy community, and missional-minded discipleship?

Rick McClain: The same line of questioning is running in my mind, "Why is there a 'disconnect' between the deaf community and the practice of spiritual disciplines?" I asked two people at a Deaf Men's retreat and they both said, "No one has told us of such." So I am going to have to wonder along the same lines of the Lord's Prayer, many can tell you it is in Matthew and Luke, but they cannot tell you what it says. They might get some of the words right. I would imagine less than one percent. Is it important? For a churchman like me, yes. But we have lost some of that priority along the years; instead of recapturing the transformational aspect of Spiritual disciplines, we are now dropping the practice because it has become "rote practice". I am hoping we can return to the value of God's word from a transformative standpoint, and not simply an informational standpoint.

Bruce Persons: Christianity has always been a creedal religion. If we depart from using creeds, which were designed to help Christians define and articulate their faith, we do so at our own peril. I am always amazed at how few people know, out of all creeds, the Lord's Prayer. The Apostles Creed is a wonderful one to use as well, with Nicene Creed expanding upon the dual natures of Christ. Like what Rick said, it must be about transformation, not simple rote practice.

It can also be a vehicle by which orthodoxy and project meets and a tool that strengthens one's faith in the Triune God. I spent most of my childhood years in a creedal denomination with Lord's Prayer, Nicene Creed, the Augsburg Confession, etc. It was not until I joined a Church of the Brethren congregation with a Deaf church when I "found" the Lord in middle school. In the first few years of my faith formation (high school), I was repulsed by the reeking scent of "dogmatism" and "religion" found in creedal denominations and longed for a simpler faith (such as that found in the Church of the Brethren congregation). Church of the Brethren, being Anabaptists, rejected almost all traditions, creeds, and confessions to restore the simplicity of the worship activity.

However, since spending a significant amount of time studying various creeds and confessions, I now realize and appreciate how valuable creeds and confessions are since they are (for most parts) rooted in the Scriptures and helps people understand their faith better. But there is always a danger of creeds losing their relevancy and power when they are recited by worshipers on a weekly basis. You bring up an interesting element here: the standardization of the Lord's Prayer. I had never considered this, and it might be helpful for some people to memorize Lord's Prayer by standardizing it!

Bob Ayres: Creeds are a key way to instruct the essentials of the faith to each new generation. The Lord's Prayer is given by Jesus in the first-person, plural (our, we, us...) implies that we say this prayer together or when privately, on behalf of others. This prayer contains praise, confession, forgiveness, request for provision, and the comfort of a child being held in the arms of a "daddy" (very personal use of the reference to God as father - Abba). My point is that reciting even this short, simple prayer together is an act of obedience, but even more... it is an instructional understanding of who God is and our deep need for God. This is one to memorize and carry with you. The other creeds are not as important to memorize as they are to recite in our worship. This is an example of proclamation in ways other than preaching. Creeds are a community-wide and universal statements about who we are and what we believe. I just wonder if integrating creeds into worship into the Deaf Church is an important practice for instructing a new generation.

Rick McClain: In order to teach the fundamentals of the Christian faith, I must have already initiated a personal relationship with the person with whom I am attempting to teach the elements of the Christian faith. We can get in the "rut" of thinking that by teaching these creeds, we can "Christianize" the new Christian. When we attempt to travel along that route, then we are "idolizing" the Creeds.

Yet, when I look at Matthew 28:19-20, I see what Jesus is implying in the process of making disciples. There is a process of conformation to the Word of God by which transformation is taking place in the new believer's life whereby the Word of God (First aspect of the Wesleyan Quadrilateral), as well as the new believer's experience of God is being taught the Faith of the New Life (This is the Tradition aspect of the

Wesleyan Quadrilateral), while he begins to define his own experiences (A third aspect), which reinforces his ability to explain (or reason out) his faith. This, to me, is the process of making disciples of all nations, which includes baptizing them in the name of the Holy Trinity, and teaching them all things we have been commanded. BUT none of this can be accomplished without an intentional relationship with the disciples.

Bruce Persons: Deaf Ministry of all denominations have been experiencing a severe shortage of ordained clergy and Deaf ministers. We often wonder how we can better reach out to those in remote locations or in areas where no Deaf church or interpreted ministry are available. While researching the Episcopalian Conference of the Deaf (ECD) of the Episcopal Church, I came across an interesting article to share with all of you. Several Deaf Episcopal Churches have been using the internet and video technology in lieu of actual priests for churches across America without a priest to conduct services and administer sacraments: "Episcopal deaf ministries continue long history of service in new ways": episcopaldigitalnetwork.com/ens/2013/07/11/episcopal-deaf-ministries-continue-long-history-of-service-in-new-ways/

Here's another excellent article written by Mark Rogers from the Gospel Coalition that explains the benefits of in-the-flesh seminary education: thegospelcoalition.org/blogs/tgc/2012/11/12/why-go-to-seminary/

Bob Ayres: I want to weigh in on the importance of theological/ministerial study for pastors and ALL ministers of the Gospel. Every profession requires standards of training and education... from the plumber to the policeman to the professor. Our Lord deserves our best and we should hold ourselves to a high standard. Ministerial training makes us more knowledgeable and well-rounded.

Rick McClain: What seems to grab my attention is that style and substance might change, but the content never does. We read a great deal about the contextualization of the Gospel for the Deaf community but it is difficult to pin down. When I served with the Ministry Strategy Committee in the Church of the Nazarene some 20 years ago, I met a woman who was a Chinese Missionary TO the United States. Her mission was to Minister to the Chinese immigrants in the US. We were working together in committee and the gist of our group conversation concluded with these words, "The contextualization of the Gospel in the ethnic context is a much more simple approach to formulate than that of contextualizing the Gospel for the Deaf and Hard of Hearing. There are a great many reasons for this discrepancy, and yet the need for cultural relevance to be applied has never been more important. It would behoove the Church in general and the Church of the Nazarene in specific to be mindful of this concept."

Noah Buchholz: Rick, why do you think that contextualizing the gospel for the Deaf and Hard of Hearing people is harder than for other cultural groups? In my opinion, it is true because there are not enough Deaf ministers and Christians who strive to truly contextualize the gospel for the global Deaf community, making the gospel sense to Deaf people. What most of us have been doing is just translating the gospel into sign language. The only difference between our *kerygma* (proclamation) and hearing American *kerygma* is different languages, sign language for us and spoken language for them. This certainly is not enough. We must not only translate the gospel into sign language but also into something that is understandable within the context of Deaf culture.

For example, after Jim Elliot and his band were speared by a group of Indians, their wives went to the group of Indians and proclaimed the gospel to them by explaining that God's only son has been speared for our salvation because spearing, not crucifixion, spoke to their hearts. What is translating being crucified as being speared equivalent in Deaf culture? To announce in Deaf people's heart language, something that is beyond native language, is to make the gospel understandable through both language and culture. This is a primary reason providing interpreters for Deaf people in a hearing church is not enough. We must come together and create a whole new kerygma, the Deaf *kerygma* that genuinely speaks to Deaf people's hearts. This means new songs, new prayers, new liturgies, new rituals, new homilies, new everything. Of course, all of them will need to work together with God's Word and the Christian traditions. We need to keep going forward and expect new things from God. We need to keep replacing old wineskins with new wineskins as God is pouring upon us new wine constantly. Thus, Acts 2:42-47 should serve as a broad guideline rather than a blueprint to be followed precisely. We must keep marching onward with Christ's love.

Rick McClain: I think we must get beyond the language of worship and move into the being of worship. The question is appropriate in that we are discussing what deaf worship looks like, instead of the emotive, auditory quality of worship. Yet, we can never fully dismiss all of the senses entirely. I think in a collaborative sense, they all are the reasons why people do return, repent, and commit to Christ.

Bruce Persons: St. Anslem of Canterbury, would say, "faith seeks understanding." Our search for knowledge must begin with our faith, not vice versa. One has to ask, what is the motive for this acquisition of knowledge? What does one do with this knowledge? Is it for self-advancement, selfish reasons, or arrogance? Or is it acquired and disseminated in a manner that serves the Church and the Body, and also equips and exhorts the saints to do greater works of ministry?

Rick McClain: Being right is only important if Jesus is at the center, not man's or culture's philosophy. The Scripture does teach we must be careful not to be syncretistic with the philosophy of man of culture as 'there is a way that seems right unto a man, but it is leading to their destruction', and therefore if we follow only the desires of our heart we will be misguided. But if we were to delight ourselves in the Lord, and there is a study worthy to be undertaken, we would come to see that ONLY His word, His plans, and His purposes are delightful and satisfying - thereby granting us the desires of our heart as He has cleanses, and provided His Grace.

Discussion Questions

1. What is a Creed? How are Creeds connected with the Bible? What value might Creeds have in teaching biblical truths? What are the concerns about Creeds?

2. What is Theology? Why would teaching biblical theology in the church be important? Is understanding Christian theology important for everyone or just the ministers?

3. What are the general concerns when a church leader lacks training? What are the dangers of inadequate training? Can theological training become toxic to ministry?

Deeper Dive: What are the barriers to church leaders receiving quality theological training? In addition to knowledge of the Bible, what other skills are important for a pastor or church leader to develop? In your experience, have most of the problems in church leadership been a result of inadequate training in theological or personal skills?

Inclusion and Recovery

Bruce Persons

In my Pastoral Theology class at Beeson, we are required to address a specific and delicate pastoral issue. Here's the case: "Address the following situation in a pastoral manner: Your key lay leader shares with you that he is gay and asks whether he should stay in his marriage." Please present your rationale (different than personal opinions) with Scriptural support, and also please respect other people's positions on this issue.

Marvella Sellers: First, PRAY for His wisdom and always be honest and thank the person for sharing a struggle – this is absolute key because that person is showing a huge amount of trust in you. Second, bring in God in this situation; pray boldly and in caring Christ-love- encourage the leader to do the same.

All through this, LISTEN to His Voice, if God is telling you to step back and arrange for his wife and you to meet first if you are their pastor, arrange other Christians to be present (ask him who he trusts with this) to partner with the wife and him to discuss this openly. Do it and arrange the meeting. If God is telling you to focus on him and his wife, ask him if he has shared this with her. If he hasn't, support and encourage him to do this- be sure to include his wife in all options in very beginning. If He is telling you that the leader is in pain (spiritually attacked, addicted to something, mental, emotional, and/or has a traumatic event in the past or present), ask him if this is the case and plan accordingly. There are many other things but I have noticed this tends to be the top three issues. Also, since he is a leader strongly advise him to take a leave from his commitments and focus on what need to be done; counseling, marriage support, and arrange for a Godly replacement for his position so he is 100% focused on the now. The verses have been given by the others in their posts. Hope this helps!

Rick McClain: The question is, can we do it without affecting our Christian testimony and relationship with others? Is Compartmentalization an appropriate response? Is it effective? Is it desirable? Does it honor God?

Bob Ayres: I believe there are at least two related issues worthy of discussion:

1) Homosexuality in the church should be discussed in the broader context of human sexuality. How do we respond to heterosexual couples living together outside of marriage? Divorce and remarriage? Serial sexual partners by single people? Adultery?

2) Social justice and equality rightly includes homosexuality but fits into a general flow of scripture related to human dignity, peace, justice, mercy, and compassion. What are the boundaries of human rights? Society sets these limits. As Christians, scripture (and arguably tradition) set our standards for behavior and expectations of justice.

Rick McClain: I have to ask if we have ever considered that as a Christian, we have the distinct responsibility - a divine responsibility, mind you, to speak the truth in love without lording over them as the pagans do. One cannot speak the truth to someone with whom there is no relationship or the perception will be that we are two-faced, no matter if we speak the truth in love. We must earn the right to speak, and to be heard. I've seen God's grace work in the lives of many people - from the liar, to the pedophile, to the sexually immoral, to the drug addict, and even to a man whose heart was full of anger, hatred and violence (me). As Paul said, Jesus Christ came into the world to save sinners, of whom I am the worst (1 Tim 1:15). That is, as Paul says, "a trustworthy saying."

Michael Gonzalez: There are many issues that can be presented but I wanted to make it short. Last semester during Spiritual Formation class at Gordon Conwell Theological Seminary, one professor told us (students) "I conducted a research by giving out a survey to men who are seminarians on this campus. After collecting the survey, 80% confessed to viewing pornography during seminary or internship. So, what are the triggers for them to view pornography?" Eighty percent are pretty large number…

Bob Ayres: Michael, you bring up a very important issue. I believe pornography is the *primary* source of poison and toxicity to relational health in our society. There has always been sexual activity and deviant behavior, but viewing people engaged in sexual acts on such a wide-scale basis has only occurred within the last fifty or so years. Voyeurism like this was previously relegated to places like peep shows, strip clubs or houses of prostitution and clearly identified as perverted. Now, even children and youth can access sexual images on their smart phones or computers.

This should greatly concern us all. What is the psychological impact of pornography on the human brain? Our brains are producing chemicals in response to these stimuli and distorting our whole sense of healthy sexual expression. There are many studies showing the link of pornography to deviancy and particularly with rape. Men who view pornography have a higher likelihood of believing that woman "want it" and ignore cues (or words) to the contrary. This is only one example. Sin is never a victimless crime.

Michael R. Gonzalez: My main focus is alcoholism. I am a recovering alcoholic and have been clean for over year. I am very thankful for overwhelming support from seminary I received and feel the need to reach out those to those whom are dealing with this addiction. I always believed that alcoholism is based on a wounded inner soul. I had to take sabbatical leave for several months to focus on my inner healing before I went back into ministry. The trigger of wanting to drink again is based on my unresolved conflict in past. So the Lord healed me tremendously, for which I am truly thankful. I am continuing to deal with difficult pain which made me into better servant for God.

I have been battling with alcoholism since I moved to Massachusetts in 2003. Deaf churches truly need to develop good collaboration with AA/NA groups where it will provide all recovery resources. There are a couple of Deaf pastors who dealt with my alcoholism. It was very awkward to them because they were inexperienced with addictive behavior and also they had a lack of resources on how to put me through a recovery program. But I am thankful one Deaf pastor was very supportive toward my recovery during my residency in Massachusetts, and we have been friends since 1999. He had experience with alcoholism, which ran in his family.

Bob Ayres: I think addiction, especially among young people... not only drugs and alcohol, but sex, porn, gambling, gluttony, gossip, even addictive attitudes of being a victim, complaining, manipulation, etc... are concrete issues for which the church can become a healing place. How active in providing support groups should Deaf Churches become? How can we become more qualified for leading these types of support groups? I see this as part of the healing ministry of the church. Should this be part of our outreach?

Rick McClain: By nature of the Cross and Resurrection, by virtue of the NEW Creation that we have experienced because of the victory that Christ gives to us, are we not to be (not become) an example of recovery? I know that there is much simplification going on, and there is much in the way of "lack of teaching of proper steps in the recovery process," etc., but isn't the Church in her true state of relationship a recovery church by existence? When I read Jesus' words in the Temple (4:18, cf. Is 11:2 - 5; 49:9; 50:4), I am thinking that BECOME is only appropriate if the Church is functioning in a manner that is different than what the Lord intended. That begs a deeper introspective reflection, "What makes a good recovery program? How does it begin; how is it lived out in daily life?" I beg that we do not re-create the pattern of the 70's & 80's where programs were the focus of the Church and not focusing on, and building upon the relationship that we have in Jesus Christ!

Michael Gonzalez: There are great concerns in Deaf churches, many pastors, minister leaders and teachers need to be more sensitive to those who are in addiction recovery. They should be willing to show respect toward others by not drinking in front of them. They are held accountable when they cause others to stumble in faith when it comes to drinking in front of them.

Bob Ayres: Here are five very interesting and challenging articles for our discussion on building healthy Christian community:

1) "Listening to Young Atheist, Lessons for a Stronger Christianity" by Larry Alex Taunton: theatlantic.com/national/archive/2013/06/listening-to-young-atheists-lessons-for-a-stronger-christianity/276584/

2) Here is a thought-provoking essay in Relevant Magazine online: relevantmagazine.com/culture/10-challenges-facing-us-next-decade

3) We need to ask ourselves the most difficult questions about what it means to be "church" in the 21st Century. "When We Criticize the Church" by Micah J. Murray: redemptionpictures.com/2013/03/22/when-we-criticize-the-church/

4) "What Non-Christians Want Christians to Hear" by John Shore: patheos.com/blogs/unfundamentalistchristians/2013/07/what-non-christians-want-christians-to-hear/ *(Thanks to Jeremy Breland for sharing this blog).*

5) "As Protestants decline, those with no religion gain" by Cathy Lynn Grossman: usatoday.com/story/news/nation/2012/10/08/nones-protestant-religion-pew/1618445/

These articles are painful to read but essential to face. In my youth, I rejected the Christian faith because of my perception of mean-spirited, hypocritical people. It was through people willing to meet me where I was, journey with me, and lead me into an uncluttered look at the gospel that I was able to grasp who Jesus is and commit my life to following Him.

Like Jesus, we journey with them towards a new reality of wholeness. Jesus met people where they were, loved them, healed them and set them on a path of healing which results in personal holiness. We all are broken by sin, redeemed by grace; God wants us to become whole. Sin breaks us and the Spirit puts the pieces back together. An environment is created for wounds to heal.

Billy Graham is quoted as saying "God's job is to judge. The Holy Spirit's job is to convict of sin. Our job is to love." I wonder if the missing part of this quote is Jesus' job: to show us how to express "grace and truth" (John 1:14).

Discussion Questions

1. How much are addiction and emotional issues—drugs, alcohol, sex, porn, gambling, gluttony, gossip, "victim" mindset, etc.—an issue in the Deaf Church?

2. Should recovery and support groups, like AA/NA and *Celebrate Recovery*, be part of the church mission? What are possible challenges of sponsoring recovery groups?

3. How do you believe the church should respond to those who are part of the LGBTQ+ community? What should the response be for others who are involved in sexual relationships outside of marriage as a commitment between one woman and one man?

Deeper Dive: Hearing churches go through difficult times when relationships are strained or unhealthy and conflict erupts, but the Deaf Church in particular—because of the smaller numbers and close-knit relationships—is impacted even more when discord arises and may even close down as a result. Are you aware of any examples? If so, do you think that a more robust support-group approach would help or hurt? How would you design such a program for a church of 10-30 members?

Digital World

Jessica Belwood

Is Facebook a good avenue to advance the gospel? In Paul's letters, we do see admonishment, encouragement, teaching of spiritual truth, but he has also said that he longs to visit with them and work out issues in person. Paul spent days, months, and years with the people he raised up. And letters were used as the LAST option to keep in touch. There is a reason Paul chose not to publish a book or just send letters to everyone instead of traveling and seeing people face to face. I believe that faith has to be caught, or else people turn into Pharisees since they have no idea what the love and sacrifice of Christ means until it's FLESHED out to them. Just like Jesus came into our world, we need to be continually IN the world with potential apostates or people who don't know Jesus. Facebook doesn't allow us to be IN the world of people- it only allows is to observe the superficial lives of people. I think working out relational issues with people is a lot scarier than participating in threads online. If people have to resort to Facebook to have their voice heard, it means they're not being heard at home. Let's all go back home. Let's all go back to the heart of community- learning to love, listen, respect, admonish, lead, and serve the people who live only miles away. I think we need to empower the local church in apologetics, healthy relational skills, leading skills, and so much more.

Bob Ayres: What do you see as the role of Vlogs/Blogs in the 21st Century Deaf Church? What are the benefits? What are the dangers? Vlogs have been great in DeafWorld but there are things that concern me as well. The best communicator "wins" regardless of the integrity of the message.

A recent vlog attacking Christianity was full of inaccuracies but many of those watching it likely accepted it as completely true. I shook my head as I watched it and imagined all the people being misinformed. The response is either to post a competing vlog disputing each point made or ignore it (both require lots of prayer). The problem with this approach is that the "other side" is defining the terms of engagement. We need to proclaim grace and truth and be careful about being put into a defensive posture.

Matthew Belwood: Some Vlogs have some great information and are pleasing to watch. But I, too, have several concerns regarding Vlogs – if some of these "Vlog sermons" were given in a church, I would hope that the elders would have stepped in to ensure the accuracy of scripture was clearly consistent with their church tradition and biblical theology. Right now, I don't see many Vlogs under the authority of church elders/deacons that take their responsibility to shepherd the flock and rightly divide the truth among the congregation. Of course, we have concerns about Vloggers who post information beyond their level of understanding and authority, but what about when the Vlogger does get the content right? Should we praise this? I've come in contact with several scenarios where the preacher/messenger will share the truth as outlined in the Scriptures, then never have contact with that young person again. Usually either the young person will have a spiritual high after receiving the truth, then come crashing down when they sin again ("Was I ever really a Christian in the first place?") or they feel the pangs of conviction, "guilted" into their realization of their depravity. Both of these situations further isolate the young person from the church/Christians ("I will never be good enough. If they really knew the sin that I did, they would never accept me.") I call this hit and run evangelism. It's a messy accident when someone tosses the truth out there and hopes it hits someone. I love the story in Acts 8 between Phillip and the Ethiopian Eunuch-Phillip heard Isaiah being heard and ran up to the Eunuch and asked him if he understood what was being read. "How can I," he said "unless someone explains it to me?" In the same way, we need to give space for people to ask questions, navigate the information, and process the experience. I personally I believe ministry happens in the flesh.

Noah Buchholz: I'm open to the idea of forming some kind of group for accountability and support. We need to make sure it will not be exclusive. We also need to remind viewers that they have responsibilities too. Maybe we need to make neutral vlogs explaining how viewers are responsible to check the sources and examine the vloggers' credibility.

Sometimes I wish I had a group of people who could check my draft vlog before I posted it on the internet. Maybe the next step is to set up a group for vloggers to simply give feedback to each other's vlogs before they are released. We can set up some guidelines explaining how to provide constructive feedback.

Todd Miller: It has always been my thought that there needs to be a fair and balanced approach to information. If one side presents information (or view/ perception), where is the other side? My church members are telling me that friends are coming up to them and saying "we have seen this vlog, and it's really made me think"... Unfortunately, those vlogs were from the other perspective. I think that the confluence of Facebook and vlogging has really exploded in the deaf community, and we need to be leading the explosion, not playing catch up. We're losing this battle for clear and rational thinking. Credibility is also an issue in how, and by whom the information is presented, depending on the audience. I love The Poached Egg site (thepoachedegg.net). It's an aggregate feed of all the various apologist blogs.

Rick McClain: Vlogs and blogs are designed to be used as they are. Essentially, they are Op Ed's (opinion editorials) and as such are not bound to rules of accountability as a newspaper column might be. Yet, in every case of writing an opinion editorial, there is always a disclaimer included that the opinion of this writer is not the expressive opinion of the newspaper. We don't see that in vlogs, nor do we see it in blogs.

We do not require that all vlogs provide an abstract whereby the author of the vlog gives a 100 word thesis to "entice" the viewer to watch the vlog. If this were done, within the parameters of a proper abstract, we might have a much better avenue to rate our viewer selection. But this is not the intent of a vlog. It is, however, the intent of every writer who submits an article for publication.

Before anyone can begin to accept accountability that comes with vlogging, the first step is to determine the PURPOSE in which the vlog is being distributed. As a consequence, the rule of free speech is the only rule of accountability for vlogs. If it is a biblical vlog, then there are other accountability issues involved. If it is political, then the rules of accountability are also defined. But for the purpose of personal vlogs, there is no boundary of accountability involved.

As with anything (books, articles, movies, etc.) there are good vlogs, and there are distasteful vlogs. What determines the value placed on these vlogs is the reviewer's opinion. Because vlogs are highly opinionated, and are viewed within the framework of opinions, there is a high degree of criticism that will be encountered. Whose opinions are right? What do we do if those opinions are not shared by everyone in the group? The consequence is what we often see in vlogs - continuous posting and re-posting of arguments of which none have anything to do with the purpose of the vlog!

For me, there are excellent vlogs. Brad Schaff and his Table-Talk Vlogs come to my mind rather quickly. His signs are clear, his production is top of the order. Other vlogs that have a more "personal agenda" are done not according to the parameters of public speaking, but according to pleasure and intent. Sometimes, people who make these vlogs are so emotionally involved that clarity has been compromised in order to deliver a particular message.

Finally, vlogs, for the most part, do not provide reasonable avenues whereby textual and historical criticism might be utilized. When I read an article, there are references to check, and recheck their sources. Editorial integrity implies that everyone understands the necessity to give credit where credit is due, and if you are paraphrasing someone else, to provide a resource/reference whereby critical review and analysis may be accommodated. However, with vlogs, this is not always available.

Vlogs that have certain prescriptive titles do provide a personal bias and experience background. There isn't much to deal with in these vlogs. Every vlog is different in its intent and purpose. It behooves the originator of the vlog to provide the substance and reason to continue to watch.

Matthew Belwood: I think you are right, a vlog would be more aptly categorized similar to an "op-ed" piece in the newspaper. It represents the opinion of the author and no one else. I think in the same vein, this could be true for several other methods of communicating, to a degree, such as Facebook status updates or tweets. It merely represents the opinion of the writer and is not necessarily in the same vein as an academic pursuit/truth.

Praise God for our Freedom of Speech. But it made me think: does that mean we are hands off in the accountability department because it represents the personal opinions of those who post these thoughts? Personally, I think in the case of those who aren't believers, I would be "hands off" myself. I don't think it is prudent to "fight back" with a video/vlog of my own (what would that accomplish except more discord?), but if it was a friend who lived in my community, I might be able to bring it up in a private, conversational context to discuss the thoughts more in-depth. I don't see my "not responding" with another vlog/video response as "giving up," though I do see it as acquiescing (as you mentioned) by recognizing that I am not in the place where I can effectively bear witness to the Light. Andy Stanley reminds his leaders often that we should "never give away influence unnecessarily." If I respond to someone's vlog with no personal connection and anyone on the World Wide Web able to see it, we are in danger of losing that influence that is entrusted to us.

But I do think that in the case of believers, we have a mandate to hold one another accountable for our actions and words. I think of Mark Driscoll saying some distasteful things on avenues that are considered "personal opinion" on his Facebook page, twitter handle and blog, and in some cases (as reported in Christianity Today), the elders would confront Driscoll for his choice of words/thoughts on the matter and Driscoll would even publicly apologize. Even though he had the freedom to express his opinion, he was still held to a higher authority.

I don't think we are exempt or not responsible for keeping others accountable, to a degree. The context of the situation is important. As we move to the 21st Century Church, and we see these vlogs, I think we need to develop a proactive approach to "responding" appropriately, both in the flesh and with our own videos.

Jessica Belwood: Intimacy will never be able to develop fully online. Interacting with people online provides many advantages. I'm quite a part of the social networking generation myself – I see the advantages but I also see huge disadvantages. I met my best friend online. I suspect this is going to become much more common in the future, although we should tread with wisdom and extreme caution. We knew each other by name online for a few years, but after we met in person (again, after much discernment of character, safety, etc) we became close. God used her as a huge source of encouragement, accountability, and support. We were able to fly a few times a year for a few years to visit each other. We met our future husbands at the same time, prayed for them together, married the same time, had our first child the same time. But as time went by, we weren't able to travel as much due to family commitments and finances, and our friendship stagnated. We remain close friends, but without the physical presence no relationship can grow deeper. I've had three long distance relationships that all stagnated after months apart, due to the lack of physical presence. My husband and I chose to have me relocate to the Midwest before we married to make sure we were making the right choice. There is so much more to the physical presence as compared to digital presence.

If we jump ahead and try to make the best of the digital age without healthy boundaries, appropriate wisdom, and healthy relationship building skills, we could crash and burn. We're the generation dying for intimacy because we feel nobody genuinely takes the time to listen to us. Would it be better to train people within the community to actively listen to each other than trying to spout off "truth" to everyone? People crave authenticity, but it is best experienced and enjoyed in person, even in a digital age.

Discussion Questions

1. What is the best way for vlogs/blogs to be used... for encouragement... instruction... evangelism... worship? What are the benefits of vlogs for the Deaf Church? What are the potential problems? How can you discern reliable and unreliable vlogs/blogs?

2. Social media brings people together but can damage relationships. How have you been helped or hurt by social media? What safeguards have you taken to protect yourself?

3. Online relationships can become pathways for meaningful, life-long friendships or give a false sense of intimacy. What are the positive and negative aspects of online interactions with people you've not met in person? What are some of the real or perceived threats of these relationships to building a local, authentic faith community?

Deeper Dive: If you were creating your ideal Deaf Church or ministry, how would you use Social Media and other technology for worship, teaching, and outreach? With this new tech-savvy generation, how do you use technology without losing the motivation for in-person interactions? What are some ideas for "live" or pre-recorded videos that could be part of the online training for members and for those outside the church?

21cDC Discussion Contributor Bios

Jessica Belwood – A daughter of the King of Kings, a big dreamer of how to better the Deaf world, Jessica believes in living life and loving as powerfully and authentically as possible. Jessica has a BA in Psychology from the University of Washington, and is founder/owner of Bellewood Virtual Assistant, where she empowers other Deaf-owned businesses to thrive through social media, marketing, and administrative support. She was involved with ministry for ten years, where she met her handsome and intelligent husband, Matthew. Jessica is the proud mother of two little boy-tornadoes, Matt Junior and Michael.

Matthew Belwood – Matt has served with Deaf Teen Quest since early 2001. A graduate of Kentucky Christian College, he holds both a BS and MA degree specializing in Youth Ministry and Counseling. In July of 2017, Matthew became National Director for Deaf Teen Quest. This was the result of a long process of discernment by Youth for Christ to identify who would lead the ministry into the future. Matthew's experience includes roles as a Deaf Education teacher, Behavior Intervention Specialist, and Adjunct Professor at Xavier University and the University of Cincinnati. He is married to his beautiful wife, Jessica, who work together to raise two beautiful young boys.

Noah Buchholz – Noah is a PhD student in Religion & Society at Princeton Theological Seminary and lecturer in the Program in Linguistics at Princeton University. Previously, he served as Assistant Professor of American Sign Language and Deaf Studies at Bethel College in Indiana for three years. Noah holds a BA from Wheaton College and MDiv and ThM from Princeton Theological Seminary. Noah is married to Alyssa and they have two daughters. In his free time, he enjoys reading, watching movies, and hanging out with his family.

Michael R. Gonzalez – Comic Geek, Coffee Addict & Avid Photographer; has been married to Tami Jo Gonzalez since 2016. He has been involved in Deaf Ministry for over two decades as a teacher, preacher & evangelist. He is an American Sign Language Mentor for Piedmont International University and teaches for Deaf Dimensions Ministry. Michael has a BA in Deaf Pastoral Studies from North Central University and MA in Educational Ministries from Gordon-Conwell Theological Seminary.

Todd Miller – Todd felt the call to serve God at a young age and at sixteen joined a traveling drama team that traveled nationally and internationally. He graduated from Deaf International Bible College with a Bachelor's degree in Pastoral Studies and served churches in Wisconsin, Illinois and Pennsylvania. Todd is currently the pastor at Connecting Deaf Fellowship, Audubon, PA. He lives in Philadelphia, with his lovely wife and three children. He is employed at The Boeing Co. and enjoys tinkering and riding on motorcycles in his free time.

Bruce Persons – As a speaker, writer, teacher, and pastor, Bruce is a Gallaudet chaplain affiliated with Christian & Missionary Alliance, founder of the Bison Christian Fellowship at Gallaudet, founding pastor of The Table Church in Frederick, MD (thetablecma.org) and blogs at brucepersons.com. Bruce is an Eagle Scout and graduated from the Maryland School for the Deaf. He holds a BA in Management from Hood College and MDiv from Beeson Divinity School (Samford University). In his free time, Bruce likes to read, watch movies, travel, read, woodwork, and loves fly-fishing, running, biking, swimming, and hiking.

Marvella Sellers – A woman who identifies as a Christ-follower above all else and adores ABBA with all of her heart and being. She thrives to honor Him through all things with the joyful delight that won her heart when she was a little girl. She holds dual BA in Creative Drama and

Elementary Education, and MA in Exceptional Education and Deaf Education, and has a special spot in her heart for hearing parents and families with Deaf/HH and DeafPlus infants up to adults. Marva works with as an Early Interventionist and Educator. A native ASL speaker of poetry and Biblical truths, her dream is to empower, encourage and enlighten people from all walks of life, languages, and corners of earth to GLORIFY God.

CHAPTER II—Narrative of Hope

Redemption and Blessing

In our first chapter, several vital issues have been identified and elevated through the insights of the Facebook discussion group. While it is important to address challenges in life with shared ideas, perspectives, and opinions—to move beyond casual and peer-informed approaches into action on critical issues requires developing a logical framework by which one makes decisions and forms opinions. In religious studies, this might be referred to as developing a *theological* (some prefer *philosophical*) perspective.

Metaphorically, in nautical terms, *theology* provides a 'gyroscope' that helps prevent a disastrous 'rolling over' of a ship in a turbulent waters and *scripture* is the main 'compass' for navigating the uncertain journey ahead and arriving at the chosen destination. Without *theological* and *scriptural* foundations for stability and direction, conclusions would be undependable and unable to withstand the tests of time. This chapter offers a theological underpinning for approaching these complex topics that is both optimistic and faithful to the historic understanding of a local, Christian fellowship.

Courage

The church universal is a calling by God, a mystery of salvation and community that puts believers on a journey of redemption from suffering. God's transformation of his people and his church into Christ's image through a relationship with this triune God is, by its very nature, beyond comprehension. The simplified imagery of the bridegroom and the bride is used by John the Baptist, Jesus, Paul, and John in the book of Revelation. The calling to this communion of believers is not so much about solving a mystery, as it is entering a journey of personal and communal transformation. Colossians 1:15-20 provides the scriptural underpinning for what it means to be a church, the body of Christ:

> [Jesus] is the image of the invisible God, the firstborn of all creation. For by him all things were created, in heaven and on earth, visible and invisible, whether thrones or dominions or rulers or authorities—all things were created through him and for him. And he is before all things, and in him all things hold together. And he is the head of the body, the church. He is the beginning, the firstborn from the dead, that in everything he might be preeminent. For in him all the fullness of God was pleased to dwell, and through him to reconcile to himself all things, whether on earth or in heaven, making peace by the blood of his cross.

Jesus is the head of the body, which is the church, and continues to reconcile humanity with himself through those who comprise the church (2 Cor. 5:11-21). This mystery of reconciliation—the atoning death and resurrection of Jesus—presents us as holy, blameless, and accepted through grace, yet includes responsive obedience. Through the incarnational presence of Jesus, faithful believers experience personal transformation. There are two parties in this new covenant: God and followers of Jesus. Grace is a gift and works of grace are a response. Maturity in a church fellowship is often linked to a deeper understanding of what God does in and through the ecclesiastical body of Christ to turn suffering into hope through the cross and empty tomb.

The history of the Judeo-Christian faith includes anguish as an expected outcome of obedience. The journey at times is bitter. Dietrich Bonhoeffer is oft quoted, "When Christ calls a man, He bids him come and die. It may be a death like that of the first disciples who had to leave home and work to follow Him, or it may be a death like

Luther's, who had to leave the monastery and go out into the world."[13] J. Oswald Sander's classic work *Spiritual Leadership* begins with two foundational principles for Christian leadership: sovereignty and suffering.[14] Jacob Spener in his introduction to the classic *Pia Desideria* alerts followers of Christ to suffering as intrinsic within an authentic experience of faith:

> [Let us remember that in the last judgment] ... we tried to edify our hearts amid the scorn of the world, denial of self, taking up of the cross, and imitation of our Savior; with what zeal we opposed not only error but also wickedness of life; or with what constancy and cheerfulness we endured the persecution or adversity thrust upon us by the manifestly godless world or by false brethren, and amid such suffering praised our God.[15]

Unfortunately, much of the suffering in the Deaf community comes at the hand of the "hearing" church through patronization, neglect, devaluation, prejudice, and other expressions of oppression. How does the church effectively face the past and present to assure a more biblical future?[16] The hope is for a more redemptive future. For example, what job possibilities exist for seminary graduates who are deaf? Are they confined solely to pastoring a Deaf church? Why wouldn't people who are deaf be considered for other positions for which they are trained and gifted within the church and academia? Could not a deaf minister serve in a large church as the director of small groups, or discipleship, or missions, and so forth? Assuming

---

13 Dietrich Bonhoeffer, *The Cost of Discipleship* (London: SCM Press, 1948/2001), 44.

14 J. Oswald Sanders. *Spiritual Leadership: Principles of Excellence for Every Believer* (Chicago: Moody Publishers, 2007), 22-23.

15 P. Jacob Spener. *Pia Desideria*, trans. Theodore G. Tappert, (Minneapolis: Fortress Press, 1964), 36-37.

16 Douglas Webster, email message to author, October 25, 2014.

this candidate is equally qualified as a hearing candidate, deafness becomes the primary mitigating factor. The unemployment rate for deaf college graduates is around fifty percent while for their hearing peers, this number is under twenty percent.[17] Does the body of Christ have a responsibility to find ways to look past differences, including deafness, and provide legitimate opportunities for qualified individuals? Technology makes this goal even more obtainable. Clearly there remains much that can be done to create opportunities for fair employment in ministry. Marginalization as a result of audism is a common experience for people who are deaf.

With suffering come hope and promise. The scriptures are full of assurances like a "peace of God, which surpasses all understanding" that guards our hearts and minds (Phil. 4:7) and scriptures like "those who sow in tears shall reap with shouts of joy" (Ps. 126:5) and the well-known Jeremiah 29:11 verse: "For I know the plans I have for you, declares the Lord, plans for welfare and not for evil, to give you a future and a hope." Throughout the New Testament, we see that Christ came to give us new and abundant life (John 10:10); he says his 'yoke is easy' and his 'burden is light' (Matt. 11:30). We are closer than ever before to a fair and just world for those who are deaf or hard of hearing.

Courage is required for those who want to move from despair to enthusiasm. Once the majesty and mystery of God's actions are realized, the journey becomes an adventure with God's Holy Spirit as a constant companion and guide. As Vernon Grounds writes, "Love, service, and faithfulness, these are God's standards and only God in

---

17 Charles Reilly and Sen Qi, Gallaudet Research Institute, accessed August 11, 2015, https://research.gallaudet.edu/Demographics/deaf-employment-2011.pdf and National Center for Educational Statistics, accessed August 11, 2015, https://nces.ed.gov/fastfacts/display.asp?id=561.

His omniscience can use these standards in evaluating the work we do as disciples of Jesus Christ."[18] Success is not measured by worldly standards and is to be considered irrelevant. Concerns shift to a deep passion for obedience. God initiates and His people respond. God's calling and mystery form and inform a journey that is brimming with possibility and wonders for all.

Calling

In his two-volume set *Living in Tension*, Douglas Webster asks a poignant question: "Have we made too much of the office of the pastor at the expense of every-member ministry and effective pastoral care?"[19] He effectively presents a supportive biblical narrative for the essential role of each member of the community of faith for proclamation, mission, and pastoral care. Webster elevates the role of the laity without undermining the importance of the clergy but warns about the imbalance that occurs when too much of a distinction is made.

Using Jeremiah as a model of calling, Webster affirms three truths regarding the priesthood of all believers: 1) there are no self-made priests; God shapes our identity; 2) there are no self-reliant priests; God defines and defends our ministry; and 3) there are no self-motivated priests; God empowers our work.[20] The calling of the pastor is to be a spiritual leader of a community of faith.

---

18 Vernon Grounds. "Faith for Failure: A Meditation on Motivation for Ministry"—TSF Bulletin, March-April 1986.

19 Douglas D. Webster. *Living in Tension: A Theology of Ministry*, vol. 1, *The Nature of Ministry: Faithfulness from the Beginning* (Eugene, OR: Cascade Books, 2012), 18.

20 Webster, *Living in Tension*, 1:20.

Spiritual leadership is one calling among many. Webster points out, "It makes good sense for a person gifted by the Spirit, trained in the Word of God, and chosen by the congregation, to take a leading role, but there is no biblical mandate that reserves these responsibilities exclusively for the pastor."[21] There is only one sacred Priest, Jesus Christ. "Since then we have a great high priest who has passed through the heavens, Jesus, the Son of God, let us hold fast our confession. For we do not have a high priest who is unable to sympathize with our weaknesses, but one who in every respect has been tempted as we are, yet without sin. Let us then with confidence draw near to the throne of grace, that we may receive mercy and find grace to help in time of need" (Heb 4:14-16).

Through the presence and leadership of the Holy Spirit, Christians serve each other as a royal priesthood. The pastor or priest is simply one role—albeit a vital one—within a diversity of giftedness. Each member of the Body has a unique calling for ministry and mission. The priesthood of believers is proclaimed in 1 Peter 2:9: "But you are a chosen race, a royal priesthood, a holy nation, a people for his own possession, that you may proclaim the excellencies of him who called you out of darkness into his marvelous light."

Pietism leader Jacob Spener emphasized the importance of the priesthood of believers, the practice of faith as evidence of authenticity (including loving one another), avoidance of religious controversies, improvement in clergy training and preparation, and the focus of preaching on essential beliefs. Spener identifies the distortion of Christian doctrine through worldly perspectives that infiltrated the

21 Ibid. 24.

Christian faith.[22] The fundamental cause for the Church losing its identity is a substitution of worldly authorities and influences. Webster provides a valuable insight that reflects similar concerns: "Never before in the history of the church has the business world governed the church world like it does today."[23] Webster points out that the salvation story begins "with the priesthood of all believers and the call of God to salvation, service, sacrifice, and simplicity."[24]

The church is finding adversaries of biblical truth externally in the secular media, entertainment world, science, and technology. There are other dangers within the structures of a church that dissuade people from discovering, developing, and using their God-given gifts for ministry. An article by Larry Taunton in the *Atlantic* magazine reports interviews with self-proclaimed atheist students on college campuses. Although many expressed respect for ministers who took the Bible seriously, their journeys into atheism centered on several commonalities: church attendance when younger, hearing vague or superficial answers to difficult questions, and the Internet factoring heavily into their conversion to atheism.[25] Middle adolescence was the common decisive time for abandoning the Christian faith. Embracing unbelief often resulted in a period of emotional distress. Taunton cites the movement away from faith as a *reaction* to negative experiences in Christianity. One negative reaction was to those who identify as

---

22 Spener, *Pia Desideria,* 51.

23 Webster, *Living in Tension*, 1:4.

24 Ibid. xiii.

25 Larry Taunton. "Listening to Young Atheists, Lessons for a Stronger Christianity," *Atlantic Magazine Online*, June 6, 2013, accessed June 12, 2015, http://www.theatlantic.com/national/archive/2013/06/listening-to-young-atheists-lessons-for-a-stronger-christianity/276584/. Interviews were with college students who were members of Secular Student Alliances (SSA) or Freethought Societies (FS). Special thanks to my colleague Jeff Heine for bringing this article to my attention.

Christians but are without personal conviction. In this post-modern age of uncertainty, even if a person disagrees with another, there remains certain appreciation for clear, personal convictions. Believers are wise to develop a stable sense of identity as followers of Jesus as revealed in the scriptures while maintaining respect for the perspectives of others.

A pastor's attentiveness to God's presence and guidance is an essential component of calling. John 15 is a rich chapter with imagery of abiding in Christ, living as part of a loving community, being courageous in the midst of adversity, and encouragement to not take this journey alone. Improved self-understanding and more honest self-examination grow out of this type of spiritual environment.[26] Disregard for these priorities will certainly lead to personal and professional difficulties that can have severe consequences.

Researcher Kirstin Stewart evaluated a number of studies from across denominational spectrums and confirms the crisis faced by churches, pastors, and other ministry staff. Thousands of pastors are terminated annually. Of those terminated, one study shows 45 percent leave church-related vocations.[27] Indications are of a significant percentage of pastoral vacancies across the denominational spectrum but particularly in smaller churches.[28] A 2004 study compared six other studies in search of a common theme for the reasons behind

---

26 Webster, *Living in Tension,* 1:99-134. Another excellent resource is Douglas Webster, *Soulcraft: How God Shapes Us Through Relationships* (Downers Grove: InterVarsity Press, 1999).

27 Kristin Stewart, "Keeping Your Pastor: An Emerging Challenge," *Journal for the Liberal Arts and Sciences* 13, no. 3 (Summer 2009): 112-127. Several studies are cited in this article.

28 Patricia M. Y. Chang, "Accessing the Clergy Supply in the 21st Century," Pulpit & Pew: Reasearch on Pastoral Leadership, Duke Divinity School, 2004, accessed June 12, 2015, http://faithcommunitiestoday.org/sites/all/themes/pulpitandpew/files/ClergySupply.pdf .

these figures. Pastors who were forced out of ministry identified several themes: they were poorly prepared, were not well connected, ignored matters of self-care or personal discipline, were placed in a dysfunctional congregation, experienced too high a personal cost, were unable to manage conflict, or simply "lost [their] way."[29] Several of these themes indicate a lack of personal support and the inherent isolation of the pastoral role. One might imagine how being deaf or hard of hearing makes this isolation even more likely. By ignoring the scriptural directives about the role of the priesthood of the believer, unrealistic expectations of the clergy are to be expected. Effective pastoral care suffers as congregants lack awareness of the importance of being 'priests to each other'. God's calling to ministry is both an individual and communal beckoning toward wholeness and holiness. Building a healthy Christian community is an essential element of ministry to the body of Christ, the church.

Mystery

As the mystery of Christ is expressed in the word and experienced at the sacramental table, the faith community referred to as "church" is to become a visible expression of the triune God. As a fellowship of believers, transformation into the likeness of Jesus Christ occurs through fellowship with the Holy Spirit. This mystery is expressed in proclamation of the word, worship, music, prayer, fellowship, service,

29 Michael Wiese, "Murmurs from the outside: What former pastors are saying to the church: Comparative Report of Six Studies on Pastoral Attrition," submitted to The Pastors Institute and Symposium, October 4-5, 2004, quoted in Kristin Stewart, "Keeping Your Pastor," 114.

sacraments, and other unknowable ways. In Colossians 1:24-29, Paul continues to expand on this mystery of being church:

> Now I rejoice in my sufferings for your sake, and in my flesh I am filling up what is lacking in Christ's afflictions for the sake of his body, that is, the church, of which I became a minister according to the stewardship from God that was given to me for you, to make the word of God fully known, the mystery hidden for ages and generations but now revealed to his saints. To them God chose to make known how great among the Gentiles are the riches of the glory of this mystery, which is Christ in you, the hope of glory. Him we proclaim, warning everyone and teaching everyone with all wisdom, that we may present everyone mature in Christ. For this I toil, struggling with all his energy that he powerfully works within me.

Paul unfolds the meaning of this mystery: Christ in us, the hope of glory. The mystery is revealed. Christ dwells in those who trust him. Therefore, Christ is proclaimed. Christ makes the word of God fully known. Truth is taught. Disciples are raised up toward maturity. Lost people have renewed hope. God's power within those who recognize his presence—in scripture, through worship, by service, in sacrament—turns mystery into revelation. All this is according to the stewardship God provides. People have been warned of the costs of ignoring what has been revealed. The Christian faith is inherently Christocentric. Christ is the Lord and center of Christianity. Any other competing gods are unacceptable. The heart of a healthy church makes its deepest commitment, extends its greatest energy, to prayerful attentiveness of this mystery revealed, Christ in us.

While there are diverse styles of worship within the Christian community, the following elements are generally included in services: reading of scripture, musical expressions, prayer, proclamation, and the sacraments. Fellowship and instruction generally occur outside of the structured worship service although elements of both are generally included. However, the primary purpose of worship is to glorify God. In the book *Center Church,* Tim Keller categorizes four general approaches he calls: Two Kingdoms, Relevance, Transformationalist, and Counterculturalist.[30] Keller identifies various traditions that also tend to share worship styles. For example, *Two Kingdoms* tend to be traditional churches that approach worship as being "for God" but basically believe religion has little to do with the rest of life. The *Relevance* "Seeker Church" movement strives to make the worship experience particularly attractive to the "unchurched" and non-Christians. Regardless of the different expressions of worship across the spectrum, there remains general agreement that worship itself is a focus on God's presence. Keller reflects on the value of insights from each of these perspectives: "A *Center Church* approach seeks to blend the cultural and biblical insights of all the models into actual practice and ministry."[31]

Preaching—proclamation of the word—is seen in many traditions as the center of worship; while others maintain the Lord's Supper or Eucharist is central. These are not necessarily at odds. Preaching should be strongly based on a proper exegesis of scripture that culminates with an invitation to the table.[32] There is a temptation to reduce proclamation of the gospel solely to preaching. Webster points out some thirty words used in the New Testament for proclamation

---

30 Timothy J. Keller, *Center Church: Doing Balanced, Gospel-Centered Ministry in Your City* (Grand Rapids: Zondervan, 2012), 231. Redeemer Presbyterian Church was established in 1989 as a Presbyterian Church of America (PCA) church plant in New York City.

31 Keller, *Center Church*, 236.

32 Douglas D. Webster, "Spiritual Theology of Christian Ministry" (classroom lecture, Beeson Divinity School, Samford University, July 8-19, 2013).

including: proclaim, announce, preach, teach, explain, speak, say, testify, persuade, confess, charge, admonish.[33] Over- or under-emphasis on the preaching of the word might even become a barrier to fuller proclamation. Preaching is only *one* way to proclaim the gospel. When churches ignore scripture, prayer, and the sacraments and reduce worship to mostly singing and preaching, the broader experience of worship is truncated. The gospel itself might even become truncated by reducing it to emotional and spiritual consumerism. Worship becomes richer when the mystery remains, and the narrative is to be experienced within the context of Christian community.

Music is the other standard aspect of church services. Without question, music exists at the heart of worship both historically and contemporarily. Inspiring music has been a central part of revivals throughout history. Even in Deaf churches, music plays a role in worship except in the most rigid settings.[34] Few hearing people really understand the lack of appeal of music to many deaf people. For the younger deaf and hard of hearing community, music videos are a staple and part of their culture. The signing technique for music is unique with larger, more dramatic motions and has historically only been done by either hearing people or deaf people who are receiving cues from a hearing person. The use of worship music videos, projected in the background, with a deaf leader signing the music in a style that resembles storytelling is a popular means to include music in Deaf worship services. As visual people, most deaf and hard of hearing people are

---

33 Webster, *Living in Tension,* 1:25.

34 Some in the Deaf community refuse to embrace any form of music as being "hearing worship." This position generally reflects the opinion of a few, older people with strong personalities. Contemporary music in worship is generally a nonissue with younger generations.

strongly drawn to dramas and interactive story-telling. This emerging technique of blending music, video, and drama has been labeled as "DraMuSign" by Chad Entinger, who says, "Drama is to deaf people what music is to hearing people."[35]

The sacraments are where heaven and earth overlap.[36] Regarding the sacraments Webster writes "It is neither mundane nor magical. This is the mystery that is filled with expressible, articular meaning. We approach the mystery of the gospel of Christ, not as a problem to be solved, but as a truth to be embraced and proclaimed."[37] St. Augustine describes the sacraments as an "outward and visible sign of an inward and spiritual grace."[38] Baptism and the Lord's Supper are the two sacraments embraced by every Christian tradition. Roman Catholicism, the most ancient Christian institution, celebrates seven: Baptism, Confirmation, Holy Communion, Confession, Marriage, Holy Orders, and Extreme Unction (Anointing of the Sick or Last Rites). While the administration and interpretation of the sacraments has been the source of great divisions in the Christian body, there is great value and meaning in these traditions of the Church. Interestingly, there seems to be a renewed interest in the younger generations in ancient and creedal traditions. The Church in this century shares a spiritual lineage that must be maintained and communicated to the next generation as part of the mystery that is Christ.

---

35 Ayres, *Deaf Diaspora*, 111. Chad Entinger is the Executive Director of Deaf Missions, an international Deaf ministry resource and training center (www.deafmissions.com).

36 Scholar and theologian N.T. Wright deserves credit for emphasizing the concept of the overlapping of these two realms and the promise of the coming heavenly kingdom. He identifies this not only in the sacraments but in the world around us.

37 Douglas D. Webster. *Living in Tension: A Theology of Ministry*, vol. 2, *The Practice of Ministry: Faithfulness to the End* (Eugene, OR: Cascade Books, 2012), 81.

38 Webster. *Living in Tension*, 2:87.

Journey

The calling and mystery now become the journey. Some may see this as a journey of individuals while others focus on the collective purposes of the church. This journey of faith includes spiritual formation and skill development. Organizationally, this body of Christ is called to create an environment of church growth, leadership development, spiritual formation, and congregational growth, both numerically and in spiritual maturity. In his book *Center Church*, Timothy Keller presents a balanced and culturally engaged understanding of church in the twenty-first century. Keller calls for a comprehensive understanding of the gospel, a vision for contextualization, and the movement of church both organically and structurally. The overriding theme is how a church can connect with a culture that is largely alienated from the gospel. Keller calls for a "faithful restatement of the gospel with rich implications for life, ministry and mission"[39] within a specific cultural and historical context as what moves a church to their unique expression of ministry. Transformational ministry occurs at the axis of sound theology, population centers, and transformational outreach into the community.[40] As Christ followers, the church is called to understand the culture in which it dwells and live out faith in a context that communicates that faith to nonbelievers.

When connecting culturally within a secular society, the temptation exists to misapply 1 Corinthians 9:18-23: "For though I am free from all, I have made myself a servant to all that I might win more of them.... To the weak I became weak, that I might win the weak. I have

39 Keller, *Center Church,* 19.

40 Ibid. 23. Expressed as "gospel, city, movement."

become all things to all people, that by all means I might save some. I do it all for the sake of the gospel, that I may share with them in its blessings." Temptation may arise to compromise the gospel, even the core identity of the Christian faith, in order to connect with non-believers. Usually, this is well-intentioned and for the sake of the gospel. Characteristic of many of today's churches, in particular those that are interdenominational, relational, and evangelical, is a desire to find points of contact which allow for relational connections with non-believers. The intention is to spread a gospel that is theologically-sound, transforms individuals and communities, and applies effectively within a specific cultural context. Keller warns readers to avoid any assumption that the Bible and culture are "relative and equally authoritative."[41] Keller references Francis Schaeffer, who wrote that active contextualization of the gospel involves "*entering* the culture, *challenging* the culture, and then *appealing* to the listeners."[42] Christians and churches are called to reach people where they are but should have no intention of leaving them there. Christ commanded the making of disciples.

Impactful churches respect cultural diversity but do so without compromising the gospel. The intention is to allow the gospel to transform the culture through the transformation of individuals. Missional churches are a contrast community and countercultural witness while engaging the society in both word and deed.[43] The culture is engaged where it is but allows Christ to transform the individuals and the culture. Keller warns readers to engage culture with "critical enjoyment and an appropriate wariness."[44] Webster states, "The vain attempt to

---

41 Keller, *Center Church,* 89-107.

42 Ibid. 116, 120.

43 Ibid. 241-2, 252-60.

44 Ibid. 109.

dress up the gospel to make it more attractive or more exciting, only defiles it. When religion is the product of human effort, it invariably moves toward manipulation, bureaucratic control, or whimsical subjectivity, cultural conformity, and false complexity."[45] Evangelical work is not just about "earning the right to be heard"[46] but sharing the whole story of God's redemptive plan and walking alongside someone who is moving from darkness to light. The spiritual reality is that the wages of sin is death, and people need to be shown the free gift of God in Jesus Christ (Rom. 6:23).

Leadership formation, empowerment, and deployment become critical priorities. Preparation involves more than training; it involves coming alongside others on the journey. This task needs to be approached comprehensively with a commitment to ancient wisdom within a contemporary context. Seminaries and divinity schools have historically adapted to the cultures and challenges of their day and are now compelled to once again involve the church more directly in the education and formation of the clergy as society moves into a postmodern era.[47] As already noted, the low ratio of clergy to churches is alarming, as are the rising rates of clergy termination, resignation, or permanently leaving the vocational ministry. This new generation of ministers (professional and volunteer) are coming of age in a highly secular culture. Many experience tremendous emotional wounding

---

45 Webster, *Living in Tension,* 2:75.

46 This is a common phrase in relational ministry with young people and originated with Jim Rayburn, the founder of Young Life.

47 This tension of the academy and the church is so consistent throughout history that I will not include a particular reference. In my own experience, I see a clear shift in theological training within the context of the local church during the early years of the 21st century. The movement is to better integrate the wisdom and knowledge of both institutions to better equip ministers of the gospel.

as a result. Holistic ministry begins with recognizing the emotional and relational needs of those who are in positions of ministry. The scriptural directive includes all mature believers in this priesthood of believers. Addressing leadership formation includes a higher level of remediation than may have previously been the case. The journey now includes caring for those who care for others.

Calling, Mystery, and Journey in Deaf Church

There has been a historic tendency in the Deaf community over the past fifty years for those who become Christians to gravitate toward more legalistic perspectives such as Independent Baptists, Churches of Christ, and other more conservative churches. With the influence of educational mainstreaming and technology, there seems to be a stronger theological "center" among more well-educated believers who may be theologically conservative but comfortable in interactions with non-Christians and Christians from other traditions. Influenced by society in general, there is movement toward liberalization in some churches and faith communities. Reflective of the Parable of the Sower (Matt. 13:1-8), some early adapters to Christianity abandon faith altogether and turn to hedonistic or other extreme behaviors as they move out of the social structures of their childhoods. Without scripturally well-grounded, accountable, and trained clergy for those who emphasize the relational aspects of evangelical ministry, this pattern of mission drift is likely to increase.

There are several other unique challenges for Deaf churches and ministries, including an underlying perception by those in the Deaf community who view hearing people as oppressors. Some in leadership of Deaf churches and ministries believe the primary task of the church is combating oppression and confront audism. In addition, there is an observable entitlement mentality which pervades many in the younger population due in large part to disability incomes such as SSI and SSDI[48] and the lack of leadership opportunities in many mainstream public schools.

Another significant challenge for those in Deaf ministry is the relationship with the interpreter community, which stands distinct as a culture of hearing people who are part of the Deaf community. They experience unusual access and influence into the personal lives of deaf people. There is a strong and organized Jehovah's Witnesses presence in the interpreting profession. However, it is widely recognized that overall, the interpreter profession is extremely liberal with a disproportionate representation of gay and lesbian interpreters. With the vast majority of deaf and hard of hearing students in mainstream settings being accompanied by interpreters throughout the school day, it is impossible to ignore both the positive and negative aspects of the influence of sign language interpreters on the Deaf community.

Education, technology, and social access are opening many doors for ministry. Focusing on Deaf ministry in metropolitan areas is an important aspect of reaching this scattered population because of the increasing number of the Deaf community who congregate in larger cities, where there are more resources and jobs. Even those who live in rural areas develop an urban mindset through public education and the entertainment media. Deaf and hard of hearing young people share significant traits in common with hearing young people in a

48 Supplemental Security Income and Social Security Disability Income. Many middle-aged and older Deaf individuals avoid these funding sources and work throughout their careers.

post-Christian society. Deaf ministry occurs within a small subgroup, which is a microcosm of the extremes found in the larger society. Equipping leaders for ministry is an essential priority. In the Deaf Teen Quest program, there is an intentional focus in leadership training on four areas: theological framework, life balance, financial stability, and practical ministry skills.[49]

Jesus told his listeners to lift up their eyes, and see the "fields are white for harvest" (John 4:35). This scripture resonates with the potential for a spiritual responsiveness of the Deaf community. This remains the *calling* by God to share in the *mystery* of Christ on a fascinating *journey* formed and informed by the Holy Spirit. The hope for the Deaf Church is to rediscover these priorities and move faithfully toward the reality that God holds for us. Apostle Paul reminds us, "How then will they call on him in whom they have not believed? And how are they to believe in him of whom they have never heard? And how are they to hear without someone preaching? And how are they to preach unless they are sent? As it is written, 'How beautiful are the feet of those who preach the good news!'" (Romans 10:14-15).

Incarnational, Transformational, Missional

The scripture is replete with images and narratives that are to be shared collectively. The Christian faith is part of a narrative that began before Adam, includes our Jewish predecessors, and continues into a New Heaven and a New Earth. One wonders why when believers gather in the Name of Christ, even in all the collective sinfulness of the

49 Deaf Teen Quest is a ministry of Youth for Christ. These training areas exist in the context of the *Five Essentials* in Youth for Christ: Wide-spread Prayer, Loving Relationships, Faithful Bible Teaching, Collaborative Community Strategy, and Adults Who Empower.

individuals, this brokenness and hurt does not increase, it lessens. By the presence of the Holy Spirit, mysteriously those who have gathered get *better* when they bear each other's burdens. Secular and non-Christian gatherings may appear fruitful for a season but true transformation only occurs through the power of God's presence. Without the spiritual center of this gathering, people are as likely as not to leave more broken than healed. This is part of the enigma of the body of Christ. When followers of Jesus abide as the branch abides in the vine, people experience healing. When people are disconnected from Christ, the branch no longer lives whether withered yet or not. This mystery applies to individuals; likewise, it holds true for faith communities.

Paul writes in 1 Thessalonians 2:8 of sharing 'our own lives' as the gospel message is given. In youth ministry, this scripture is often cited as foundational for *relational* ministry. Relationships are established with nonbelievers as a means of building enough credibility to share the good news of Jesus Christ. There are potential misunderstandings and abuses of such a simplified understanding of ministry. Paul refers to a deeper mystery: "Christ in you, the hope of glory" (Col. 1:27). When one responds to Jesus and receives forgiveness for sins, the Holy Spirit begins to dwell within, and through believers, reaches others. This concept is a foundational understanding of *incarnational* ministry. God is the one pursuing lost people, and the task of the individual or ministering body is to remove barriers. The prophet Isaiah predicted, and John the Baptist proclaimed his mission to enter a wilderness full of lost people to "prepare the way of the Lord" (Isa. 40:3-5). The task of followers of Jesus is likewise. Incarnational ministry is being willing to bring God's presence to others through loving relationships.

When Christians enter the world of lost people full of grace and truth, it is the Spirit of Christ who actually interacts with the spirits in them. The responsibility of the church is to go in obedience. The church becomes salt in a world that has lost flavor and light in a world of darkness. The Holy Spirit convicts of sin; the task of the Christian is simply to be honest. The Holy Spirit draws lost people to God. God formed them and loves them more than can be comprehended. The task of the Body of Christ is to go in the world and to share honestly about struggles, personal experience, scripture, what has been learned, and the hope found only in Jesus. The mystery is Jesus. He is the center of our faith and forms his followers more and more into his image. Faithfulness to Christ is not about "trying"; faithfulness is learning to recognize the Shepherd's voice and to respond. As Chambers wrote about ministry for those in depression, "No preaching of the gospel of good cheer will touch that; it is only the great life-giving, life-imparting Christ who can touch it."[50] The primary challenge of the church is to avoid becoming one of the barriers to "the way of the Lord" instead of helping prepare the way. The burden of the Christian is to avoid getting in the way of the movement of the Spirit. Joy is found when followers of Jesus experience being used by God for the sake of others.

Once the reality of 'Christ in us' is recognized, the process of personal and communal transformation increases. Jesus calls and nets are dropped. It may feel like the beginning but for God it is a fulfillment of what he has been doing from the moment of conception. In many traditions, baptism marks this initial awareness of Christ that results in a personal commitment. For other traditions, infants are marked as belonging to Christ through baptism as an acceptance of God's grace.

50 Chambers, *Workmen of God*, 70.

Regardless of the method, mode, and timing of baptism, Jesus beckons to come and follow. A long journey begins. What started as stumbling steps of a spiritual child—when well fed and cared for—results in running "with endurance the race that is set before us, looking to Jesus, the founder and perfecter of our faith" (Heb. 12:2). As believers increasingly are formed into the image of Christ, new levels of healing and holiness are discovered. Eugene Peterson writes "the work of the Holy Spirit is forming our born-again spirits into the likeness of Christ."[51] The *mystery* of how change actually occurs is through the transformational experience of 'Christ in us' through the person of the Holy Spirit. God does the work of salvation and sanctification by abiding in Christ; growth occurs through submission and obedience.

Transformation does not occur in a vacuum; Jesus established the church as a tangible expression of his mission. Christians are called to live as part of a body of believers. Jesus emphasized the importance of living in community in many ways but none more succinct than: "For where two or three are gathered in my name, there am I among them" (Matt. 18:20). Acts 2:42-47 describes a transformational community who met together daily, devoted to the "apostles' teaching and fellowship, to the breaking of bread and prayer." In the same way that the mystery of 'Christ in us' transforms individuals, 'Christ in us' collectively transforms the body of believers into a missional community. This formation process finds completion as a transformed group of followers of Jesus begins to impact the surrounding community through humble service, compassion, and sharing of God's redemptive story.

---

51 Eugene Peterson, *Practice Resurrection: A Conversation on Growing Up in Christ* (Grand Rapids: Eerdmans, 2010): 2, quoted in Thaddeus Barnum, *Real Identity: Where Bible and Life Meet* (Wesleyan Publishing: Indianapolis, 2013), 59.

Far too often Christians assume that programs of the church are the ministry. In reality, programs simply create opportunities for ministry to occur. Faithful programming creates a space for the Holy Spirit to move. Personal ministry can occur, at least for a time, without programs or organizational structures. Programs actually become barriers to ministry when they occur in a vacuum void of meaningful relationships. Music may be well prepared, sermons insightful, setting bright and inviting, yet if the hearts of the congregants are cold and untransformed, more damage will occur than good, especially for the spiritually immature or visiting unbelievers. A newcomer's negative initial impression might become a permanent impression of the church experience. Programs should not become a substitute for authentic ministry, which includes the loving presence of a redeemed people gathering in the presence of the risen Lord and caring for the lost and brokenhearted stranger.

In the words of Oswald Chambers, it is essential to rely on the leadership of the Holy Spirit: "as to what to say in every case of every soul that comes… rely on the Holy Spirit for guidance."[52] Pope Francis writes, "The Holy Spirit is the soul of the Church, with His life-giving and unifying strength. Of many He makes a single body–the mystical Body of Christ."[53] Therefore, the reliance is on the Lord and not the skills of individuals.

If a church focuses on incarnational and transformational experiences without moving into service and missions, their community will eventual sour. The narrative of scripture from Abraham and Sarah

---

52 Chambers, *Workmen of God*, 11-12.

53 Carol Kelly-Gangi, ed., *Pope Francis: His Essential Wisdom* (New York: Fall River Press, 2014), 27. Quoted from his address to the cardinals on March 15, 2013.

until the end of time is a covenant for God's blessings to a people with a requirement to bless others. This has been evidenced throughout the Old and New Testaments. Ignoring the missional call of Christian community is simply unfaithfulness.

As those who serve the One True God, who has redeemed humanity through the sacrifice and resurrection of Jesus, who continues to live in believers through the Holy Spirit to comfort, heal, strengthen, lead, and convict of sin, the responsibility of the church is intrinsically evangelical. In a world with so many lost and hurting people, who desperately need the salvation and hope found only in Jesus, the calling is not ambivalent. Jesus gives a startling and convicting parable in Matthew 25:31-46 regarding the final judgment, with clear examples of the importance of caring for him through how the needy are cared for. The parable proclaims the consequences of not doing so. A transformed, missional community must weave into their lives a passion for the lost and hurting or else they run the risk of becoming a religious, members-only club. Both the prophets and Jesus blasted those who created barriers between people and God. In word and deed, the call remains for the Deaf church to remove such hindrances.

Discussion Questions

1. How does suffering lead to hope and why does it take courage to lead change? If you are Deaf, would you ever consider a ministry role in a church that is not directly related to Deaf ministry? Why or why not? For hearing people, what is your perspective of this possibility?

2. Jacob Spener describes the calling of the church: 1) every Christian is a minister, 2) authenticity is vital 3) controversies will destroy 4) training of Christians is a priority, and 5) preach on the essential beliefs. All are important but put these in what you see as "most to least import" order. Explain why you chose that order.

3. Paul writes in Colossians 1:27-28: "To them God chose to make known how great among the Gentiles are the riches of the glory of this mystery, which is Christ in you, the hope of glory. Him we proclaim, warning everyone and teaching everyone with all wisdom, that we may present everyone mature in Christ." What does this tell us about our theology and practice of ministry?

4. How do you approach the tension of authentically relating to and caring for non-Christians while maintaining a strong, personal commitment to your Christian faith?

5. How would you describe an "incarnational" faith that draws others to Christ?

Deeper Dive: Incarnational, Transformational, Missional... Explain the difference between Church programs and ministry? How do they intersect to bring about transformation of individuals and outreach to non-believers?

CHAPTER III—Ministry in Context

Oppression does not define the Deaf Community yet it must be acknowledged and addressed in any serious book about Deaf Church in this society. Some may be concerned about a *Liberation Theology* consuming the Deaf Church when such topics are brought up. This is a legitimate concern but not something expressly promoted by this book. Drs. Ayres and McClain hold to what is known as *Biblical Theology*, which thoughtfully recognizes the contributions (and weaknesses) of other theological approaches that primarily emphasize historical contexts, word interpretations, systematic scriptural themes, textual literalism, or social liberation as a benchmark of salvation. However in contrast, *Biblical Theology* scriptural interpretation is defined by the original intent of biblical writers under the inspiration of the Holy Spirit, which leads to orthodoxy in beliefs and behavior.

This chapter considers the process of moving from the theological framework into the practical application of determination of the essential values, salient challenges, and societal context of ministry in the Deaf Church. Therefore, it is appropriate to begin with an exploration of various aspects of oppression and audism and utilize them as vital lenses by which we sift through the symptoms present in current day settings. The remaining part of the chapter gives detailed information about the scope and sequence of the think-tank process on addressing current-day issues.

A Legacy of Oppression

Understanding and addressing current challenges in Deaf ministry can only be accomplished by recognizing the long history of oppression of the Deaf community that continues to be a reality of daily life. This painful legacy is briefly described here but reflects a long narrative of injustices and abuses that—while things have improved—are still evident today. Historically in the Church, much of this oppression was the result of a skewed understanding of what Paul wrote in Romans 10:17: "So faith comes from hearing, and hearing through the word of Christ". This was fueled by a widespread misunderstanding of the theological writings of the influential St. Augustine of Hippo, who at one time identified deafness along with other infirmities as the result of the sins of one's parents. For over a thousand years, there were widely held religious views that people who are deaf were both uneducable and unable to experience salvation at all, due to the inability to *hear* the "word of Christ"[54] and having a condition that prevented the physical *ability* to "confess with your mouth that Jesus is Lord" (Romans 10:9).

Augustine later wrote very positively for the deaf with regard to Romans 10:17 saying the inability to hear is only a *hindrance* to faith or an *obstacle* to communication which could be overcome through physical, manual expressions (i.e. sign language). In later writings, based on his actual, personal interactions with deaf people, Augustine affirmed that "bodily movements ... gestures ... signs" are a legitimate means for communicating and understanding the Christian message. Augustine wrote that sign language could transmit the gospel effectively.

Cleve and Crouch expand on this positive viewpoint by citing a conversation between Augustine and Evodius in chapter 18 of *De quantitate animae liber unus*. They summarize this interaction:

> In this discussion Augustine points out that he believes that deaf people can learn and thus are able to receive faith

54 John V. Van Cleve and Barry A. Crouch, *A Place of Their Own: Creating the Deaf Community in America* (Washington, DC: Gallaudet University Press, 1989), 4.

> and salvation. This passage from Augustine also is revealing because it shows that, as early as the fourth century of the modern era, sign language ... was used by some deaf people and that it was believed to be capable of transmitting human thought and belief. Indeed, Augustine implies that it is equal to spoken language in its ability to reach the "soul."[55]

Augustine's insights regarding the potential role of manual communication are truly remarkable; yet, over a thousand years would pass before any identifiable education or ministry for the deaf would exist. Unfortunately, the earlier mishandling of scripture became the prevalent view and was used as a justification for abuse and neglect.

Pedro Ponce de Leon, a Benedictine monk in Spain in the sixteenth century, was the first known educator who believed deaf children were able to learn through manual communication and established the first school for the deaf. His contemporary, Gerolamo Cardano, a mathematician, physician, father of a deaf son, and friend of Leonardo DaVinci was the first scholar to claim deaf people could learn without first possessing the ability to speak. Other than the children of the wealthy, for the next two hundred years those who were deaf were still largely relegated to the fringes of society. Most received little or no socialization and no formal education.[56]

For the past few centuries, the Deaf community has enjoyed a rich Christian legacy mostly in relation to residential settings such as monasteries or other institutions. Modern education of deaf children originated in France during the eighteenth century by a Roman Catholic priest, Charles Michel De L'Eppe, who developed a system

---

55 Cleve and Crouch, *A Place of Their Own*, 4.

56 Julie A. Herrmann, "Communicating in Silence: The Benedictine Roots of Deaf Education," *Journal of Education and Religion* 29, no. 1 (March 2006): 163-177.

of standardized signs and finger spelling. In many ways, education developed in the context of a concern for Christian ministry for children. Many of the state residential schools for the deaf were begun by ministers or sons of ministers.[57]

In 1817, Reverend Thomas Hopkins Gallaudet, along with Deaf French educator Laurent Clerc and Dr. Mason Cogswell (father of a deaf daughter, Alice), co-founded the first educational institution for deaf children in North America. Rev. Gallaudet became its first principal.[58] Gallaudet was mission-minded and evangelical as is evidenced in his sermons yet likewise focused on the perceived outcome of Christian conversion – the civilization of those who "know little or nothing of the social, intellectual and moral enjoyments which we prize as among our highest privileges."[59] Benjamin T. Conner references an 1819 sermon at a prayer meeting connected with a mission's conference:

> Drawing on the recently rediscovered missionary text Matthew 28:18-20 (particularly the phrase "Go ye, therefore, and teach all nations") Gallaudet was compelled by an "obligation," "an imperious duty" grounded in the "explicit command" of Jesus to evangelistically educate the deaf. Our obligation as people whose ancestors were enlightened by the truth of the gospel, he argued, is to convey that knowledge to the heathen world. In this address, Gallaudet clearly casts his vision for Christian mission and evangelistic proclamation as having a civilizing function, where civilization is understood in terms of his experience of society in the United States.[60]

57 Elaine Costello, *Religious Signing* (Toronto: Bantam Books, 1986), x.

58 www.asd-1817.org/about/asd-history, accessed June 25, 2019.

59 Benjamin T. Connor, *Disabling Mission, Enabling Witness: Exploring Missiology Through the Lens of Disability Studies*, (Downers Grove: IVP Academic, 2017), 76.

60 Ibid. Connor references: Thomas H. Gallaudet, *An Address, Delivered at a Meeting for Prayer, with Reference to the Sandwich Mission, in the Brick Church in Hartford, October 1,*

Gallaudet University in Washington, DC, was originally established for teaching the Bible[61] and is now the world's premier liberal arts university specifically for Deaf and Hard of Hearing students.[62] The first Deaf church in America, St. Ann's Episcopal Church, was established in 1852 by Rev. Thomas Gallaudet, who was the son of Rev. Thomas Hopkins Gallaudet and brother of Edwin Miner Gallaudet, the founding superintendent of Gallaudet University, which was named after the elder Thomas. In 1876, Rev. Henry Winter Syle became the first deaf priest and was ordained at St. Stephens Episcopal Church in Philadelphia.[63] Before entering the ordained ministry, Syle was a Chemistry and Physics teacher, and competent in Latin, Greek, French, German, and Italian. Syle, a Methodist originally, was not allowed to pursue ordination because of his deafness. Rev. Thomas Gallaudet, his Episcopal contemporary, introduced him to the possibility of ordination as a minister. By the end of the nineteenth century, the Lutheran church launched four full-time missionaries to the Deaf. During the middle of the twentieth century, several denominations developed ministries with the Deaf community including the Assemblies of God, Southern Baptists, and Churches of Christ.[64]

1819 (Hartford, CT: Lincoln and Stone, 1819), 8.

61 Costello, x.

62 "Mission and Vision Statement," Gallaudet University, accessed on June 12, 2015, https://www.gallaudet.edu/about_gallaudet/mission_and_goals.html. The charter for Gallaudet was established in 1864 by an act of Congress and signed by President Abraham Lincoln.

63 William Stephens, "A sermon preached in St. Stephen's Church, Philadelphia, Sunday, October 8, 1876 : on occasion of the ordination of Henry Winter Syle, M.A. as deacon in the Protestant Episcopal Church," Gallaudet University—Deaf Rare Materials, accessed June 12, 2015, https://archive.org/details/gu_sermonpreache00stev/.

64 Jack Gannon, *Deaf Heritage: A Narrative History of Deaf America* (Silver Springs: National Association of the Deaf, 1981), 16, 181-183.

Unfortunately, these past two centuries of Deaf education and ministry are also replete with abuse and oppression of the Deaf community. One glaring example is Lawrence Murphy, a priest who taught at St. John School for the Deaf in Milwaukee, who for almost a quarter of a century molested over 200 boys at the school. Murphy died before formally facing justice. The Diocese of Milwaukee paid out over twenty-nine million dollars in restitution and filed for bankruptcy protection in 2011.[65] This level of abuse might be extreme, but sadly not uncommon nor reserved for Catholic boarding schools. Deaf children are more vulnerable than hearing children to sexual predators in their family and neighborhood because they are perceived as easy targets with limited ability to communicate to authorities. Beyond the issues of molestation, the sense of rejection is often accentuated by experience in church. Few churches have interpreters and even if they do, a deaf adolescent has little motivation to become involved with hearing peers because of communication barriers. The deduction from young people is often: "God is a hearing God; hearing people do not know sign language; God does not understand my language or even care; religion is for hearing people."

This historic experience that includes both oppression and more recently great opportunity encourages consideration of "the nature of human flourishing and the reality of being deaf… [is it] a disability that is redeemed or a gift that is defended?"[66] The understanding of Deaf ministry as being to a cultural, linguistic people group is

---

65 Carey Lodge, "Clergy sex abuse claims drive Archdiocese of Milwaukee to file for bankruptcy," Christian Today, published August 25, 2015, accessed October 8, 2015, www.christiantoday.com/article/clergy.sex.abuse.claims.drive.archdiocese.of.milwaukee.to.file.for.bankruptcy/62952.htm.

66 Douglas Webster, email message to author, October 25, 2014.

well-established and widely accepted. Yet, is deafness itself something to be defined as a disability to be medically "cured" through technology or science?[67] Within the Deaf community, there is no consensus on this topic other than such a decision is an individual choice. Scripturally, deafness is considered a disability which is included as part of those whom Jesus would heal (Luke 7:22). Included in this passage are the blind, lame, lepers, the dead, and the poor. The common denominator is that their condition puts them at great personal and social disadvantage which Jesus could resolve through healing. Without question, the prevailing view within the Deaf community—a view held by the authors of this book—is that "deafhood" is a gift to be defended against audism, oppression and colonialization. Paddy Ladd describes the term in the introduction to his seminal work on the topic:

> Deafhood affirms that how we have been these past 120 years is not all that we truly are. It affirms the existence of a Deaf sense of being, both within the individual and throughout the collective, which, like a river surging against a dam, cannot rest until it can find a way through that will take it down to a sea of life, where all human souls are enabled both to find their fullest self-expression and to interpenetrate each other. [68]

Interestingly, when Jesus heals a deaf man—the only passage containing details of healing a deaf person—Jesus took the man aside privately before healing him (Mark 7:31-37). What was the reason for this? Was Jesus determining whether the man wanted to be healed? Would this man losing his deafness isolate him from his extended deaf family and community, or would being able to hear introduce

---

67 i.e. cochlear implants, stem cell treatment, surgery.

68 Paddy Ladd, *Understanding Deaf Culture: In Search of Deafhood* (Clevedon, England: Multilingual Matters, 2003), 4.

him into a new, much larger "hearing" fellowship without a downside? Jesus asked the invalid lying beside the pool of Bethesda directly if he wanted to be healed (John 5:1-17). Jesus never seems to have healed someone against their will. Jesus might have gestured or even signed his inquiry to the deaf man in Mark 7 because of his knowledge of populations of deaf people who could communicate among themselves. Although it may seem surprising to the general hearing population, most deaf people *who identify as part of the Deaf Community,* do not have an interest in being able to hear. One common point of theological conversation in the Christian Deaf community is whether Deaf people will hear when they get to heaven. The opinions are mixed. Deaf identity and the visual language of signs are highly valued. When "all tribes and peoples and languages, standing before the throne" (Rev. 7:9, 14:6) is mentioned, there is no doubt in anyone's mind that this multitude includes the deaf, as a people group, praising God in sign language. Because of the richness of language and friendships, deafness is experienced as a gift to be defended. This perspective would likely be different for someone whose hearing loss was a journey into isolation. The challenges of hearing loss are related primarily to communication barriers and common experiences of marginalization, exclusion, or oppression. Possibly, the answer lies in the tension itself, between being considered a disability and a gift.

Value of Think-Tanks for Research

The declaration and call to the Deaf Church was generated by a think-tank brought together and facilitated by Bob Ayres with the ultimate goal of coming to agreement on a public declaration designed to prompt introspection, conversation, and positive insights leading to action within Deaf churches and ministries. The methodology for this group—guided discussion and overall consensus—was purposeful for modeling the value of group facilitation on any topic of importance. The collective wisdom of those concerned with any topic elevates the individual insights of all involved in the process. Think-Tanks serve as a legitimate form of practical, academic research. Involvement in this process provides participants with an educational model which can be replicated in their own ministry settings. Additionally, productive interactions between colleagues from different ministries help develop future connections for collaboration. Members of this think-tank share a common recognition of the need for dramatic changes in current practices while remaining steadfast on the essential elements of the historic, biblically-based, Christian faith.

The primary context for ministry focuses on a largely non-Christian, post-modern generation. Major influences of this generation include technology, entertainment media, cultural urbanization, racial/ethnic diversification, secularization of public education, governmental benefits, secular perspectives on sexual standards, and growing societal distaste for religion in general and evangelicalism in particular. The Deaf community is widely diverse and scattered; therefore the topic of ministry ought to include the entirety of the socio-economic spectrum and consider large geographic areas where Deaf people live and work. The praxis focused through the lens of ministry within a society that is largely defined by secular media, urban intensity, and broad technological influences.

During this process, several questions were explored: What are the essential characteristics needed for the Deaf church millennials to reach younger generations? How can a broadened understanding of the gospel proclamation that includes scripture, art, symbolism, creeds, and sacraments be developed that might appeal to future generations? How do churches effectively reach a spiritually lost, scattered generation of deaf and hard of hearing young adults and integrate them into Christian community? What are new ways to move forward within denominational expectations and potential constraints? Is a community-wide, interdenominational church a viable alternative? Is there a need for a separate Deaf denomination or network of like-minded churches across denominations? The overarching question considered was: "How do we reach, disciple, and empower these next generations of deaf and hard of hearing individuals (and communities) with the life-transforming, eternal gospel of Jesus Christ?"

Now we face the new challenge and responsibility of effectively reaching out to non-believers and caring for those who come to faith in Christ. How shall we respond to a resurgence of faith in the Deaf Community? Will we learn our lessons from mistakes of the past? Will we reclaim our right to follow Jesus as we discover him in the scriptures and through Church traditions without coercion or external pressure? Will we adequately care for the depressed, the confused, the immoral, the broken, the distraught soul with compassion and not criticism? The gospel is eternal but the context is always changing. How well are we contextualizing faith in today's secular environment without compromising the faith "once for all delivered to the saints"?

21cDC Think-Tank Process

In February 2014, Bob Ayres met with colleagues Matthew Belwood, Liz Martin, and Dr. Rick McClain to identify potential participants for a gathering to discuss this topic at length, referred to throughout the book as a "Think-Tank". Fifteen people who were known by us were identified and invited to a colloquium on this topic in Louisville, Kentucky. Twelve of the fifteen invited were able to attend for two full days to identify the "unique challenges" of Deaf Churches and Ministries and the "essential values" of fruitful and sustainable ministry in the context of a highly secularized culture. Eleven of the twelve initial participants confirmed to make a second trip to Louisville in February 2015 to create a one-page "Declaration to the Deaf Church" document.

Due to the consensus nature of this project, it is relevant to know more about the specific participants. The titles, positions, and locations listed are listed as at the time of the meetings. For several of these people, their current roles have changed.

- Bob Ayres (KY)—National Director, YFC Deaf Teen Quest
- Matt Belwood (KY)—Associate National Director, YFC Deaf Teen Quest
- Noah Buchholz (NJ)—Director, Deaf International
- Mary Beth Cantrell (FL)—Student, Gordon-Conwell Theological Seminary
- Joe Dixon (OH)—Pastor, Signs of Grace Deaf Church
- Chad Entinger (IA)—Executive Director, Deaf Missions
- Michael Gonzalez (IN)—Student, Gordon-Conwell Theological Seminary.
- Lamonte Grant (MA)—Pastor, Immanuel Deaf Church
- Stephen Hause[69] (MD)—Pastor, In His Hands Deaf Ministry

69 Stephen Hause was part of the colloquium but was unable to attend the second gathering.

- Rick McClain (MD)—Pastor and Adjunct Professor
- Todd Miller (PA)—Pastor, Connecting Deaf Fellowship
- Bruce Person (AL)—Student, Beeson Divinity School
- Marva Sellers (IN)—Volunteer, YFC Deaf Teen Quest

(standing l-r) Joe Dixon, Lamonte Grant, Todd Miller, Rick McClain, Bruce Persons, Matthew Belwood, Michael Gonzalez, (sitting l-r) Noah Buchholz, Chad Entinger, Bob Ayres, Mary Beth Cantrell, Marvella Sellers and Stephen Hause (not pictured).

Participants in the colloquium came from eight different denominations. Nine Caucasians, one African-American, one Latino male and two white females were part of this colloquium. This representation is not as diverse as might be ideal but there were several priorities to be considered in addition to being known by us: educational background (with the intention of including some without advanced degrees but possessing rich, practical experience), age, geographic diversity, family background (born in hearing or deaf families), educational experience (attended mainstream or residential schools), and communication preferences (American Sign Language, blended ASL/English, Signing/Oral). The group was comprised of confessing Christians with well-thought out beliefs that are not at either extremes of fundamentalism or liberalism. All have shown passion for the Deaf church in evangelism and discipleship of youth and young adults.

Our first full day was focused on identifying the challenges facing those seeking involvement in the Deaf Church today: Where are the weaknesses? What prevents healthy communities of faith to emerge? Where are these barriers coming from: both internally or externally? What factors keep the Deaf Church from truly thriving and, in many cases, not even surviving?

Our goal was to be completely honest with each other (and ourselves) without letting these topics become an excuse or cause for blaming others. Many of these problems do come from a legacy laced with oppression but our goal was to name the issues and generate ideas for overcoming the negative. These problems are real, raw, and often the result of others but we must always be wary of using them as an excuse for giving up or giving in to marginalization.

The second day was shifting the focus towards a path forward. What should be our guiding principles for church health? How do we apply these insights into a strategic approach to building healthy Deaf churches? Are there specific priorities that should be applied into any Deaf ministry setting regardless of other variables (e.g. numbers, maturity of members, region, strength of the local Deaf community). Deaf people have the same rights as anyone to freely worship, serve, and grow in faith in the context of an organized church. What are the factors preventing spiritual wellness in the church? How should we approach these challenges? The first step in overcoming barriers is to clearly identity the problems that are common in churches today.

The following three sections identify the barriers common in Deaf churches and ministries and offer a framework for addressing and overcoming common issues: 1) challenges and barriers, 2) essential values, and 3) ministry priorities.

The bold words summarize the topic as determined by think-tank consensus. The paragraph following the topic is the effort by the authors to provide further explanation.

Challenges and Barriers

Consensus was reached on twenty-one unique challenges for the Deaf Church and Deaf Ministries in hearing churches:

- Lack of resources and training
- Disunity and division
- Primary identity not in Christ
- Inward-focused patterns
- Negative images of Christians
- Irrelevance of the gospel
- High-drama toxic people
- Lack of strategic vision
- Emotional fragmentation
- Personality disorders
- Few male lay leaders
- Lack of generational Deaf families
- Need for inner spiritual healing
- Divisions by our differences
- Subjugation of the Deaf Church

- Underserving Deaf Plus/Deaf Blind
- Lack of consistent discipleship
- Conflicts created by misinformation
- Theological confusion and error
- Non-traditional sexuality and gender
- Isolation and lack of a support system

Lack of resources and training. Few viable ministry resources are available or accessible for Deaf Church leadership including effective ministry training programs. Fortunately, this lack of training and resources is improving primarily in several denominational settings. Deaf Missions (deafmissions.com) offers some of the strongest inter-denominational training and resources. Many Deaf churches and ministries rely on adapting resources developed for the general public to fit the need of Deaf/HH individuals and groups. There remains a significant lack of high-quality, useful resources and educational options for Deaf Church and Ministry leaders.

Disunity and division. The willingness to live with "secondary-issue" theological differences and collaborate across denominational lines has dramatically improved over the previous two decades. However, there remains clear separations between denominations and a lack of productive cooperation. Success often breeds an increase in egocentric leadership. The misperception of "God is blessing us so therefore we must be doing things right... and don't need anyone else" is a common trap. The blessings of God compels us to be a blessing to others. The lack of sustainability of many Deaf Churches is a reflection of the pride that perpetuates disunity.

Primary identity not in Christ. One's identity as a Christian—first and foremost, regardless of all other connections—is in response to the person, message, and works of Jesus as revealed in the Bible. Our common experience as a redeemed people is evidenced through a vital sense of unity amidst diversity. One's Deaf Cultural distinctiveness does not supplant identification with the broader Body of Christ. Development of a strong sense of Deaf Cultural identity as a committed Christian may be a priority, but when any cultural, social, racial, ethnic, or linguistic experience overrides primary identity in Christ, unnecessary conflicts emerge and unproductive divisions grow.

Inward-focused programming. Technology brings people together yet often creates even greater isolation than in earlier days. Many young people avoid important social interaction because of obsessive use with technology and media. Social media provides a false sense of intimacy and can quickly injure or destroy relationships and reputations. In a recent study of the counseling issues of undergraduate college students, dramatic increases in anxiety and isolation have been recorded. Isolation, in particular, took a sharp and steady increase since 2007, which coincides with the advent of the "smart phone" and related interactive social apps.[70]

Negative images of Christians. The general perception of Christians in our country has become increasingly negative, especially as evangelicalism has become more closely identified with conservative politics.[71] Many blame the perceived liberal bias of the judicial system

---

70 Presentation by Dr. Ernesto Escoto, director of the Counseling and Wellness Center at the University of Florida, Spring 2018.

71 Frank Newport, "2017 Update on Americans and Religion" (Gallup), December 22, 2017, accessed on July 24, 2018, https://news.gallup.com/poll/224642/2017-update-americans-religion.aspx.

and popular media. Others fault organized Christianity for a legacy of injustice: slavery, racism, hypocrisy, abuse, and institutional greed. Ephesians 6:12 says our battle is against "...the spiritual forces of evil in the heavenly places." Regardless, we live in a society that often recoils from expressions of religious faith, and in particular, those who claim to be Christian.

Irrelevance of the gospel. Pew Research Center confirmed a growing disinterest in any religion that now reflects the views of about one-third of our general population. This group overwhelmingly believes religious groups are obsessed with power, money, rules (control) and politics.[72] As is widely recognized, the Deaf Community is even more secular than society at large and many perceive church as not only irrelevant but oppressive. The Christian message as presented seems difficult for people to apply to real life and has not been experienced as something clear or compelling. There remains little motivation to become part of a faith community.

High-drama toxic people. The church was established by Jesus as a place to find hope: emotional healing, friendship, knowledge, and guidance. St. Augustine is credited with saying, "Church is not a hotel for saints, it is a hospital for sinners." However, this means the spiritually vulnerable and the emotionally contagious are in regular contact. Oppressed communities tend to have higher incidents of physical, emotional, and sexual abuse, which can lead to increased unhealthy interactions. The Deaf Community is no exception. As a result, the spread of toxic influences within a small group can quickly overwhelm and repel the more stable participants.

---

72 "'Nones' on the Rise", Pew Research Center polling on Religion and Public Life, October 9, 2012, accessed on July 24, 2018, http://pewforum.org/2012/10/09/nones-on-the-rise/.

Lack of Strategic Vision. The Deaf Church has a tendency for copying the current practices of hearing churches or unquestioningly following the Deaf church traditions of the past. Keeping current of trends and continuing traditions is helpful but can cause either blurred vision or church vertigo. Blurred vision is a misdirected focus on what worked in the past (but may not now) and church vertigo is the result of rapid and ill-conceived change. Every church and ministry has a unique calling. Prayerful, intentional, and communal decisions about how to reach, disciple, and empower church participants is a challenge for church leadership.

Emotional fragmentation. The emotional stability of many individuals in our society has been impacted by relativism, which tends to lead to compartmentalization of identity and values. Reality becomes as one determines it and may change depending on who he or she is with. Previous generations recognized personal hypocrisy as an internal conflict in values, yet current ones perceive various personas as expressions of the same, complex self. This fragmentation of identity, compounded by entertainment and social media, creates new challenges and opportunities for the churches to develop meaningful mentoring, discipleship, and socialization activities.

Personality disorders. These are characterized by 'deeply ingrained patterns of thinking and behaving that generally lead to impaired relationships. Mental health professionals formally recognize three general types of personality disorders, although each exists on a spectrum: odd/eccentric disorders, (paranoia, schizoid, and schizotypal personalities), dramatic/erratic disorders, (narcissism, histrionic, and borderline personality), and anxious/fearful disorders, (avoidance, dependence, and obsessive-compulsive personality)'.[73] Deaf church leadership face these same types of personality disorders in their membership but with fewer resources for serving them.

Few male lay leaders. The absence of committed adult male leadership in many Deaf churches is a challenge. Although most churches have male pastors, it has proven difficult to raise up strong male leadership due, in part, to the lack of positive role models and mentors. *Deaf Diaspora* describes the "Missing Generation" in the Deaf Community as those born during the 1960s and 1970s who largely abandoned church due to societal and educational secularization which created a vacuum of Christian role models.[74] Many pastors have little or no training in relational outreach for connecting with males in the community. In a post-modern society, few people will come to church activities unless first meeting somewhere else more neutral.

Lack of generational Deaf families. One of the realities of Deaf Churches is the lack of multiple generations of church membership. Around 90% of deaf and hard of hearing children are born to hearing parents and the vast majority of Deaf/HH parents give birth to hearing children. In contrast with the hearing church, generation-to-generation Deaf families as the long-term foundation of a Deaf church is almost impossible to maintain. As hearing children become adults and have their own families, they tend to move into hearing churches, if they attend church at all. Vibrant youth ministry programs that attract new families to the Deaf Church are rare.

---

73 Summarized from *Psychology Today* website, accessed on July 24, 2018, https://www.psychologytoday.com/us/basics/personality-disorders.

74 Ayres, *Deaf Diaspora*, 34.

Need for inner spiritual healing. Though not unique to the Deaf Community, there is a widespread emotional and relational brokenness in our world that is expressed in toxic and addictive behavior. The church is charged with creating a healing community of faith where unhealed wounds and deadly addictions can be addressed and helped. The reality is that the source of much of this dysfunction is spiritual in nature with feelings of having no hope, worth, or purpose. Healing these most basic issues of the soul are the only way to really change behavior. The church is charged with a "ministry of reconciliation" to bring transformation and renewal.

Divisions by our differences. "And if a house is divided against itself, that house will not be able to stand" (Mark 3:25). Not only does an inherent cultural dynamic exist between Deaf and Hearing participants, but there is often a tension between generations, ethnicity, and morality. Deaf Churches may become unwelcoming to outsiders who are notoriously sinful or awkward in a church setting. Spiritual pride may exhibit itself through behaviors such as shunning, gossiping, controlling, divisiveness, or hostility. At the heart of judgmentalism is a devaluing of others who are different; not 'welcoming the stranger' as described in Matthew 25.

Subjugation of the Deaf Church. The Deaf Community has a legacy of subjugation by the hearing world and continues to be a marginalized and oppressed people group. While there has been progress, oppression takes many forms and can become a defining issue. When repression—real or perceived—becomes internalized, other problems emerge such as passivity, depression, implosion/explosion, entitlement, or abdication of personal responsibility. Oppression can come from a variety of sources and is complex. Discussing issues of marginalization and resisting oppression may be ignored until emotions become raw and relationships are hurt. Though not often discussed, marginalization may originate from within the Deaf community itself and can become destructive and divisive.

Underserving Deaf Plus/Deaf Blind. The Deaf Community is as diverse as the hearing world, included various experiences of deafness and of differing communication needs and preferences. Approximately 10% of Deaf/HH individuals have physical and/or cognitive disabilities (referred to as "Deaf Plus"). Some Deaf individuals have Usher Syndrome or other visual impairments. Accessibility to language for all creates a challenge that can be overlooked and underserved. For those with cognitive challenges, there may be a pattern of being devalued. Deaf Churches tend to serve their membership well but few have an intentional outreach to the Deaf Plus and Deaf Blind.

Lack of consistent discipleship. Much of the growth in Deaf Churches has occurred in the more conservative, evangelical denominations. Because of their emphasis on conversion theology and evangelism, intentional steps of discipleship may be lacking. Churches with catechism provide a formal program of orientation to the Christian faith but often have little beyond the initial program that tends to be for adolescents. Intentional discipleship and mentoring exists is some churches but is not commonly seen outside of the Sunday morning service. Programming discipleship runs the risk of devaluing the essential relational components as modeled by Jesus. The challenge is to move beyond didactic instruction and into small groups and/or one-to-one mentoring.

Conflict created by misinformation. One of the challenges of living in a world with persistent communication barriers is the *gaps in* *information* that occur daily. As a result, it requires additional effort to fully understanding a topic or event. As a result, rumor and misinformation can spread quickly. Pastors and church leaders are compelled to remain informed and mediators of information. Many Deaf churches lack the foundational leadership for noticing, intervening and navigating misleading conversations, especially when they take place online, by texting, or through email. This dynamic can cause a vulnerability that collapses a church from a single incident.

Theological confusion and error: Theological training opportunities for the Deaf/HH pastors and church leadership are few and far between. Qualified, well-equipped, and properly educated pastors within Deaf churches are lacking in number. Gaps in biblical knowledge and historical foundations can lead to a sketchy theology that is inconsistent or even unbiblical. With the post-modern perspectives of moral and social relativity, there is a spread of a theology influenced by a culture that rejects all authority, whether it is biblical, historical, or traditional. Poorly qualified but highly capable ASL communicators can mislead church attendees with questionable theology with an emphasis on the narrative without proper understanding of the metanarrative of scripture, including its authority.

Non-traditional sexuality and gender: One of the major challenges of this generation for all churches and denominations is how to care for those living outside traditional sexual patterns. Many churches have rejected any outreach to those in same-sex relationships although generally many individuals in the churches have gay and lesbian friendships. Few transgendered individuals see the church as a safe place to visit and explore the Christian faith. Many young people see nothing wrong with living together in a sexual relationship before marriage.

The challenge for the church is to meet people where they are while maintaining a loving and faithful biblical witness.

Isolation and lack of a support system: Lastly, the persistent isolation of Deaf ministry continues to be a major issue. Isolation is the bane of Deaf Ministry. In the Deaf Church and Ministry, we are plagued by the lack of peers and colleagues who challenge and encourage us. Most Deaf pastors struggle to find a local support system even if they are part of a larger hearing staff. Fortunately, over the past two decades, the situation has improved with travel and technology. Christian leaders' conferences and retreats are available across the country and organizations are making it a priority to collaborate with each other. The scattering of the Deaf Community continues to present significant challenges related to ministry in isolation.

Essential Values

Every organization or project should operate under broad values that are held up as essential. These provide a framework for tasks and help alert participants when things are getting off-track. Consensus was reached on four foundational values identified as essential for the Deaf church:

- Healthy relationships
- Effective discipleship
- Innovative worship
- Impactful outreach.

Healthy relationships. The church should be a place of healing, forgiveness, and Christ-centered love. People are attracted to authenticity, kindness, acceptance, and hope. Jesus' prayer for his followers was to "love each other" and become one body, which is how others know he came from the Father (John 17:22-23). Far too many people have been hurt in the church through abuse, neglect, gossip, bullying, and legalism. Jesus established the church to be a place of healing, hope, and service. For the Deaf Church to thrive into the future, the foundational fruits of the Spirit described in Galatians 5:22-23—love, joy, peace, patience, kindness, goodness, faithfulness, gentleness, self-control—should define us as brothers and sisters in Christ and by what others observe about us as followers of Jesus.

Effective discipleship. More resources need to be adapted to best fit a Deaf cultural setting. Discipleship begins with church leadership, which includes the pastor, and calls members on a lifelong journey of accountability, mentoring, and training. Without discipleship and spiritual formation, pastors become performers, members become spectators, and outsiders are left without a place to belong. What exactly are we calling people to, if there is no cost or commitment involved? Jesus commanded us to go and make disciples. Conversion is part of the discipleship process, where at some point, the individual becomes aware of the tugging at their heart by the Holy Spirit. Effective training and discipleship of adults, especially in this generation, requires a discussion-based instructional methodology that includes formal and informal settings that are working from the relational groundwork of the Christian faith.

Innovative worship. The post-Christian culture of today is quite similar to the environment of the first-century church. Acts 2:42-47 provides a basic model of teaching, fellowship, prayer, and the breaking of bread as four essential components for experiencing *koinonia* (deep, committed fellowship) within a potentially hostile culture. Several biblical elements, including preaching and music (or drama), become important aspects of meaningful worship. The worship experience in the Deaf Church needs to be culturally appropriate and innovative with care not to simply copy the hearing worship modalities. Jesus models excellence in Deaf Cultural worship in his use of instructional dialogue, participant inquiry, interactive learning in context, leadership empowerment, "storytelling," and outreach into secular environments.

Impactful outreach. The covenantal legacy of the Christian church was first given to Abraham and is God's promise to bless his people so they will be a blessing to others. This concept of sharing the blessings of life with others resonates well with the younger generations. The Millennials are particularly interested in seeing *evidence* of generosity and mercy in a nonjudgmental context as a precursor to openness to any system of belief. They have little trust of authority or logic but place their confidence in experience. Few people realize that social ministry—visiting the sick, feeding the hungry, visiting those in prison, and so forth—are part of the evangelical expressions of the church. Historically, caring for the outcasts in the name of Jesus went hand-in-hand. To reach the next generations of Deaf/HH young people, the church must learn to value and combine both social and evangelical aspects of ministry.

Ministry Priorities

One way to think of ministry priorities is as the *essential values put into action*. What does it mean to follow Jesus? How does a church body know when they are on-track with the calling of Christ for his

Church? Consensus was reached on ten ministry priorities identified as essential for the Deaf church:

- Incarnational ministry
- Prayer
- Inner healing
- Transformation
- Contextual teaching
- Formation
- Missions
- Support networks
- Service
- Unity

Incarnational ministry. Colossians 1:27 proclaims the "mystery, which is Christ in you, the hope of glory." This scripture points to one of the key theological points that is often overlooked: it is God who works in and through us for impacting others. Our responsibilities are to abide in Christ, care for others, and let the Holy Spirit work. Just be honest when non-believers ask you questions about your life and faith. It is God doing the work; we are just vessels who help prepare the way of the Lord. This is the mystery, Jesus is in you. Incarnational ministry is mostly just showing up and being obedient. Therefore, the power of the church is best expressed with the grace and truth of Jesus Christ. You cannot effectively share Jesus with others unless you have earned their respect and hopefully, their trust. Caring for others is vital in being faithful to the church's calling as the Body of Christ. The Lord is present (incarnate) when we gather in his name. The Lord is present (incarnate) when we read scripture, proclaim his word, and in the sacraments. This is what incarnational ministry means; because Christ is in us, transforming us, and we are able to be tangible expressions of the Body of Christ. Which brings us back to the importance of clean hearts, grace-filled spirits, forgiven souls, and actions that reflect Jesus. Incarnational ministry is a priority of building a healthy church.

Prayer. Jesus prayed without ceasing and the Apostle Paul reminds us in 1 Thessalonians 5:16-18, "Rejoice always, pray without ceasing, give thanks in all circumstances; for this is the will of God in Christ Jesus for you." How can the expectations we have of God be fulfilled without talking to him? How can God's expectations of us be accomplished without going to him regularly, consistently, in prayer? Yet all too often, prayer seems to be a low priority or an afterthought. Every relationship depends on communication. As a church, we need to incorporate prayer on a much deeper level than is commonly practiced in many churches. Worship can be experienced in a number of ways but none more intimate than prayer. Prayer can be part of outreach: "Do you mind if I pray for you?" After the 9/11 terrorist attacks, Youth With a Mission (YWAM), set up a series of booths on street corners near Ground Zero marked "Prayer Station" and offered to pray with passersby. This was well-received and picked-up by the national news. The YWAM-ASL in Washington, DC later became very involved with "David's Tent"; a non-stop, interdenominational prayer initiative for our country that began on September 11, 2015. Creative expressions of worship and prayer can edify the church body, minister to others, and provide fuller exposure to an authentic worship for new and non-believers.

Inner healing. This generation shows significant emotional wounds, and the church leadership is wise to become more skilled and knowledgeable in providing places of healing. Forgiveness—both the act of being forgiven and forgiving others—is a unique contribution to the world by the Judeo-Christian tradition. Giving and receiving forgiveness has been recognized and promoted throughout the mental health field as an important therapeutic process. The church of today can become a safe place for lost and broken people to find inner healing through the hope found only in Jesus Christ. Followers of Jesus are called to journey with others through support groups, counseling, accountability, mentoring, and prayer. One of my favorite instructional exercises when teaching is to gather with the class in a comfortable place, such as a coffee shop, and say, "Behind every scar on your body is a story. Let's go around and each person pick a scar on your body and tell the story behind it." Everyone has at least one scar and can recount their story in vivid detail, including the time, place, emotions, level of pain, who was with them, and so forth. Then I ask a series of questions beginning with "what is the difference between a wound and a scar?" The questions are intended to help connect the process of the physical care and healing of a wound (that if cared for properly, becomes a scar) with proper emotional healing. Through our physical bodies (and in the world around us), God provides us many real world examples that guide us towards wholeness and reconciliation. Inner healing occurs best in the context of safety, honesty and authenticity.

Transformation. "Do not be *conformed* to this world, but be *transformed* by the renewal of your mind, that by testing you may discern what is the will of God, what is good and acceptable and perfect." (Rom. 12:2) For many, the church experience is one of trying to *conform*—playing the "church game" and fitting in—instead to where the scripture points us, something much deeper: to *transform*. Through faith, in response to God's grace, we begin a journey from one existence into another. We change. All things become new. We begin the process of becoming more like Jesus. The Greek word used here is *metamorphoo* which is where get the English word *metamorphosis*; such as a caterpillar becoming a butterfly. The Church is called to be the vessel where the Holy Spirit brings about real change in our lives, not just improved behavior. Being "transformed by the renewal of your mind" moves beyond "what God can do *for* me" to "what God can do *through* me for others." Grasping the importance of transformation compels us to look more closely at our church programs. Is there a clarity that personal conversion is only the beginning of the journey of faith? Are we providing spiritual mentors who spend time with newer believers? Are we truly engaged in discipleship or just teaching content? Are we responding to God's call to reform the consumer mentality through the cultivation of a spirit of prayer, humility, unity and service?

Contextual teaching. "To the weak I became weak, that I might win the weak. I have become all things to all people that by all means I might save some. I do it all for the sake of the gospel, that I may share with them in its blessings" (1 Cor. 9:19-23). Adapt your content and signing to fit your audience. Youth and young adults, in particular, learn best when able to engage in dialogue; younger children need more interactive "hands on" learning. Instructional technique is only part of the contextualization. Information that engages the emotions better informs the mind. Jesus would often tell a story or parable that made his point. He was the master of asking probing questions to teach when he already knew the answers. How you ask a question makes the difference between people parroting answers (whether they believe them or not) and looking introspectively for deeper comprehension and application. Building a strong biblical foundation for faith remains the duty of the church leadership. The primary goal of teaching is for learning to occur. Are learners making sense of this information? Will it apply to their context? Are we meeting in the right place or should we go off-site? How can I help them integrate this into their spiritual formation? Instruction is most effective through authentic relationships, discussion-based small groups, and in the proper cultural context. Didactic teaching methods seem largely ineffective with younger generations.

Formation. Christian formation is a descriptive term often used in liturgical churches to describe the process of discipleship. Catechism is the initial step of structured formation that through a format of questions and answers, provide a summary of the foundational beliefs in the Christian faith. Yet structure without authentic relationships based on Christ-like character can become destructive. Formation is much more than just acquiring knowledge. Jesus modeled a journey of formation as he prepared his disciples for bringing his message to the world. When Jesus first called the disciples to follow him, two of them asked where he was staying. Jesus responded, "Come and you will see" (John 1:39a). The invitation is to enter into an *authentic relationship* that answers the immediate question of lodging with a clue about the life-changing journey ahead. Formation is the process of being the disciple, not only learning what the disciple learns. Teaching, relating and encouraging the discovery of being is more significant than the process of doing. We become shaped into the calling that fulfills our life's purpose. Jesus tells us in John 15 that we are to remain attached to God, like a branch to a vine, or else little else remains. Formation is relational as well as instructional; it involves the heart, mind and hands. We are formed through authentic, Christ-sharing relationships and need a series of mentors along the ways. There needs to be both a local (internal) and global (external) focus to formation that takes us inward to contemplation and outward to service. Formation is where grace, faith, and works are integrated into a practical way of life that points others to Jesus.

Missions. Missions is inseparable from the theology of the Trinity. As Christians, we are part of the missional legacy of bearing the message of God's redemption of the world—through the power and presence of the *Holy Spirit*—that the Kingdom of our Lord has come, yet is not fully come. In Acts 1:8, Jesus promises the Holy Spirit to empower his followers to "be my witnesses in Jerusalem and in all Judea and Samaria, and to the end of the earth." The early church lifted up the name of Jesus, served the needs of others, and created new communities of faith. Involving people directly in missions is an essential part of church faithfulness and being "salt and light" in the world (Matthew 5:13-16). Christian theology holds to the belief in the Trinity—Father, Son, and Holy Spirit—as expressions of his one triune nature that is omnipotent, omniscient, and omnipresent. Jesus, "the image of the invisible God, the firstborn of all creation" (Col 1:15) is an expression of God from the beginning (John 1:1-18). Missions is more than good works, it is fulfilling our theological framework for missions: "For God so loved the world, that he gave his only Son, that whoever believes in him should not perish but have eternal life. For God did not send his Son into the world to condemn the world, but in order that the world might be saved through him" (John 3:16-17).

Support networks. Finding appropriate levels of personal and professional support is a persistent challenge for the leadership of Deaf churches and ministries. Building regular networking friendships with colleagues for nurturing and support is vital and without these relationships, people tend to spiral into depression and addictive behaviors. Through reliable friendships, we gain new and helpful insights into life. Many marriages in ministry have been saved by wise input from friends and mentors and many times this involved encouraging the ministry leader to find professional counseling. Simply knowing you are not alone in facing life's challenges of parenting, marriage, work, ministry, and whatever crises might occur makes a dramatic difference in one's ability to cope. When we started Deaf Teen Quest in 2000, one of the first tasks was to send out a national appeal for "anyone who loved Jesus and Deaf Teenagers" to gather for a symposium on how to better reach young people with the gospel. There are friendships and ministry collaboration that came out of that meeting in February 2001 that continue to this day. We need each other. When we come together as brothers and sisters in the name of Jesus, great things happen. As a small, scattered people group, there emerges a particular importance in connecting across communities, denominations, and interdenominational ministries for resources, support, friendship, and mentoring.

Service. Jesus stood in the synagogue and read from the prophet Isaiah: "The Spirit of the Lord is upon me, because he has anointed me to proclaim good news to the poor. He has sent me to proclaim liberty to the captives and recovering of sight to the blind, to set at liberty those who are oppressed, to proclaim the year of the Lord's favor." He sat down to teach and proclaimed, "Today this Scripture has been fulfilled in your hearing" (See the full story in Luke 4:16-30). So here is the first pronouncement by Jesus of his, and our, marching orders. We serve with Jesus to "proclaim good news to the poor... liberty to the captives... sight to the blind... liberty those who are oppressed... the Lord's favor." Followers of Jesus are called to engage society with a proclamation of freedom. In Matthew 25, Jesus also takes this challenge deeper to include care for the *hungry, thirsty, stranger, naked, sick,* and *prisoner*. How we treat the least and lowest among us is how we treat Jesus. Being a Christian is a mysterious mix of grace, faith, and works; every follower is compelled to grapple with the issues of faith in action. Good works do not earn our salvation but without them, James, the half-brother of Jesus tells us, "For as the body apart from the spirit is dead, so also faith apart from works is dead" (James 2:26). More than at any point in history, the Deaf churches of this generation that thrive, will hold a high priority on serving others.

Unity. In the late evening before Jesus was crucified the following morning, he prayed with the disciples (John 17). He prayed that we love one another and remain united in him: "I do not ask for these only, but also for those who will believe in me through their word, that they may all be one, just as you, Father, are in me, and I in you, that they also may be in us, so that the world may believe that you have sent me" (John 17:20-21). Unity does not mean uniformity; we are given the right to understand and apply scripture differently with integrity. But disagreeing does not mean we have permission to be vindictive. Without unity across the Christian body, there is little hope of fulfilling Jesus' prayer for us. Unity brings the church closer to what Jesus meant when he said, "your kingdom come, your will be done on earth as it is in heaven." Social injustice, expressed as marginalization and oppression, are enemies of unity. Our mandate is to fight for safety, respect, and dignity of all people. Tensions will persist and re-emerge in our fallen world, but we serve a God who requires us to love one another, even those who persecute us. Now is the time for bold, prayerful moves in response to the changes in society and need for renewal in the church. But as we do so, we are wise to keep our eyes on the guiding principles of love, respect, and unity.

Discussion Questions

1. What do you see as the primary challenges facing the Deaf church today? Give some examples of church that you think are particularly good models?

2. All of the following aspects of "being church" are important but which one do you see as of *primary* importance? Explain your perspective.

- Meaningful Worship/Praising & Honoring God
- Social Justice/Serving Others in Jesus Name
- Evangelism/Reaching Others with the Gospel
- Sound Theology/Preaching & Teaching

3 As we place an emphasis on loving people and creating welcoming environments, how do we also communicate the non-negotiable truth of the gospel?

4. What do you think of the concept of an interdenominational church? Could such a model work effectively over the long run?

Deeper Dive: Is there a need for some type of "Deaf denomination"? If there is a need for distinct denominational identity, how do we avoid the pitfalls and destructive elements of historical denominationalism? What are these elements? How do they fit within the concept and perspective of the 21st Century Deaf Church? What about an interdenominational network of like-minded churches for training, support and accountability? Knowing that the Deaf community is a tightly-knit, relationally-oriented community, how do you avoid the emergence of "cliques" that might undermine healthy growth and outreach?

CHAPTER IV—Declarations and Call

The *Declaration to the Deaf Church* is the one-page summary of fourteen-points that has been divided into two sections: a) values that should be foundational in any church including the Deaf Church, and b) values and priorities specifically applicable for the Deaf Church or Deaf Ministry.

A *declaration* is a statement proclaimed publically, usually by a small group of people, which is designed to make others aware of particular issues, concerns, or beliefs. A *call* provides explanation and offers clarity of the urgent need for specific change. For example, Jesus *declared* the temple had become a 'den of thieves' when he kicked over the tables, but issued a *call* in the 'sermon on the mount' where he described living faithfully and invited people to do so. Every 'follow me' said by our Lord was a *call* and most of his interactions with the Pharisees and Sadducees were a *declaration*.

In this chapter, the 'Declaration' is the consensus of the think-tank and is followed by the two-part 'Call' which is the work of the authors. As this book is specifically for Deaf Churches and Deaf Ministries, Drs. Ayres and McClain write with the assumption that the majority of the readers of this book are believers in Christ and likely involved in ministry. Therefore, little effort is made here in providing additional explanations of terminology or expanding upon contextual background for those unfamiliar with scriptural references or Christian theology.

DECLARATION TO THE DEAF CHURCH

As those identified first and foremost as followers of Jesus Christ, we ask our brother and sisters in ministry with deaf and hard of hearing people to join us in renewing a commitment for Deaf churches and ministries to be:

- Christ-centered
- Biblically faithful
- Full of grace and unity
- Responsive to the Holy Spirit
- Be a place of healing and hope
- Reflect God's love, mercy and justice
- Share Jesus through service and words

As those specifically serving in the ministry context of Deaf churches and ministries, we call for a commitment to:

- Spiritual freedom from past, present, and future oppression
- Build bridges for healing and restoration
- Advocate against all oppression
- Empower the Deaf community to serve and lead
- Interactive fellowship, instruction, and worship
- Embrace the marginalized in both Deaf and Hearing worlds
- Consistent awareness of diverse language backgrounds to ensure the message of the gospel is equally accessible to all

CALL TO THE CHURCH

When Jesus announced his mission, he stood up to read from the book of Isaiah: "The Lord's Spirit has come to me, because he has chosen me to tell the good news to the poor. The Lord has sent me to announce freedom for prisoners, to give sight to the blind, to free everyone who suffers, and to say, 'This is the year the Lord has chosen.'"

As your brothers and sisters, we call for all churches and ministries to renew our commitment to remain:

Christ-Centered

"[Jesus] is the image of the invisible God, the firstborn of all creation. For by him all things were created, in heaven and on earth, visible and invisible, whether thrones or dominions or rulers or authorities—all things were created through him and for him. And he is before all things, and in him all things hold together. And he is the head of the body, the church. He is the beginning, the firstborn from the dead, that in everything he might be preeminent. For in him all the fullness of God was pleased to dwell." *Colossians 1:15-19*

Jesus is the center of our faith

Whenever a faith community or belief system rejects Jesus as the literal "image of the invisible God"—the incarnate Lord providing historic expression of God our Creator, Messiah, and ever-present Spirit—that community, however religious, has diverted from the historic, biblical Christian faith. The birth, death, and resurrection of Jesus, who is Christ our Savior, is the apex of our Christian belief structure. These congregations who teach differently may be full of kind, intelligent, and generous people, but their theology departs from

Christianity. We are a Christocentric religion based on a preeminent Messiah—the historic Jesus of Nazareth—who exists eternally as "the head of the body, the church." For the Deaf Church to thrive in the twenty-first century, the centrality of Jesus remains our primary reason for gathering, worshiping, and serving.

This does not mean the our only conversations in the Deaf Church revolved around the person of Jesus, but that the heart of our message draws people to Jesus as he is lifted up in Word and Sacrament. As mentioned in the previous section on missions, emphasis of a Trinitarian understanding of God is essential. The Trinity (God in Three Persons) connects us with the entire narrative of the scripture from Creation to The Fall to Covenant to Law to Incarnation to Redemption to anticipation of a New Heaven and New Earth. We are a covenant people fulfilling promises made to God in ancient times and we eagerly make new commitments that move us into eternal life. Ultimately, all scripture, history, and tradition points us to Jesus Christ as is the center of our faith.

Love Jesus deeply. Even for those born into Christian families, baptized, confirmed, and part of a church, at some point we have to "own" our faith—even a faith with doubts—and realize we really DO believe in a God who was revealed in Jesus and pursues us through the Holy Spirit. We begin to realize, this is not just my parent's faith, or my mentor's faith, or my pastor's faith, it is MY faith. "...because, if you confess with your mouth that Jesus is Lord and believe in your heart that God raised him from the dead, you will be saved" (Rom. 10:9). Jesus is not just someone to "know about", but someone with whom to experience a personal relationship; one that transforms us into a new creation.

Biblically Faithful

"All Scripture is inspired by God and is useful to teach us what is true and to make us realize what is wrong in our lives. It corrects us when we are wrong and teaches us to do what is right. God uses it to prepare and equip his people to do every good work." *2 Timothy 3:16-17*

Scripture defines our beliefs

God has given us the scriptures as the final authority in all matters. God also inspired the scriptures to be written through human beings, who are fallible and imperfect, as a means of keeping us from turning the Bible into an idol. There are other religions who treat their sacred books as untouched by human hands in authorship. As a result, their sacred texts become indurate in a way that elevates them to the status of holy artifacts, in and of themselves, as though they are untouchable and impervious to criticism or contextualization. The Judeo-Christian understanding of the Bible is one of inspiration by God of individuals, which communicates essential truth across a variety of epochs, languages, cultures, and contexts. This keeps our focus God's pursuit of lost and broken humanity, as consistently evidenced in the Bible from Genesis to Revelation, instead of the more static view of the narrative as simply ancient texts.

Jesus is the center of the biblical narrative because God expressed himself in history as a flesh-and-blood human—the Incarnation—results in our reconnection with God because of Jesus' sacrifice on the cross and bodily resurrection on the third day. This act of atonement (reconciliation) made it possible for a Holy God to have restored fellowship with unholy humanity. All scripture points towards Jesus as the essential, culminating point in history. Jesus is 'God who became flesh' and deserves our highest adoration. When preachers say the

"Word of God" they are often referring to the Bible. But the Bible itself tells us the "Word" (*logos*) referred to in the Holy Scriptures, is Jesus. "In the beginning was the Word, and the Word was with God, and the Word was God … And the Word became flesh and dwelt among us, and we have seen his glory, glory as of the only Son from the Father, full of grace and truth" (John 1:1,14).

At the same time, we are clearly *People of the Book* in the spiritual lineage of our Hebrew predecessors and must remain committed to the inspiration, authority, and legitimacy of the texts. Even though we may have various interpretations of the same scripture passages, ultimately all scripture is inspired by God serves as the final, inerrant authority in all matters of the Christian faith. The historic creeds are 'statements of faith' based on the biblical narratives that are designed to provide clarity and share our historic, orthodox beliefs. The Holy Bible, inspired by the Holy Spirit, provides all we need for foundational theology of the Deaf Church in the context of a highly secular society.

Grace and Unity

"Since God chose you to be the holy people he loves, you must clothe yourselves with tenderhearted mercy, kindness, humility, gentleness, and patience. Make allowance for each other's faults, and forgive anyone who offends you. Remember, the Lord forgave you, so you must forgive others. Above all, clothe yourselves with love, which binds us all together in perfect harmony. And let the peace that comes from Christ rule in your hearts. For as members of one body you are called to live in peace. And always be thankful." *Colossians 3:12-15*

Full of grace and unity

Grace is forgiveness and acceptance—completely undeserved—given freely by one to another. God is the source of all grace and expressed this remarkable gift beginning with God's response to the disobedience of Adam and Eve. Although there were severe consequences for their sin, God's posture was to provide a way for them to survive and remain in relationship with him. He clothed them, sustained them, and provided a way for them to work the soil and fill the land with descendants. The ultimate redemption of humanity is grace made possible through the life, death, and resurrection of Jesus Christ. Our separation from God was removed by the goodness of God through no merit on the part of humanity. This is grace; it is a gift given freely by God to us. As those who have received God's grace, we are compelled to be full of grace for others. We reflect the values of God by showing forgiveness and acceptance of others.

Grace is the wellspring of unity. Unity is the means by which the Holy Spirit transform lives. John 13:34-35 records Jesus proclaiming, "A new command I give you: Love one another. As I have loved you, so you must love one another. By this everyone will know that you are my disciples, if you love one another." Apostle Paul uses the image of a physical body to show how the church must function; each body part has equal importance for the functioning of the entire body. "If one member suffers, all suffer together; if one member is honored, all rejoice together. Now you are the body of Christ and individually members of it" (1 Cor. 12:26-27).

Unity is only possible if grace in relationships is regularly both given and received. Unity implies that there is diversity in your congregation. Diversity without unity is explosive and will lead to fractured fellowship and hurt relationships. However, unity without diversity is ineffective. There needs to be differences in the church that would cause tension in the world. Having a group of people who look and think alike is actually unhealthy. With Christ, we become diverse and unified; accepting our differences and loving each other anyway. Although protecting unity seems obvious to what it means to 'be church', protect unity by expressing grace generously.

Holy Spirit

> "If you love me, obey my commandments. And I will ask the Father, and he will give you another Advocate, who will never leave you. He is the Holy Spirit, who leads into all truth. The world cannot receive him, because it isn't looking for him and doesn't recognize him. But you know him, because he lives with you now and later will be in you. No, I will not abandon you as orphans—I will come to you." *John 14:15-18*

Responsive to the Holy Spirit

The Holy Spirit is fully God—as Jesus is fully God—and an essential part of the Trinity; God is One God who is eternal Creator, Redeemer, and Sustainer. How God can be One, yet expressed as three "persons" is an essential mystery of the Christian faith. We are not able to comprehend this mystery but cannot reject it and remain identified a Christian. The fullness of God—Father, Son, Holy Spirit—is in all three expressions of God. When you see God the Father, you also see the Son and Holy Spirit. When you see Jesus the Son, you see the Father and Spirit. When you see the Holy Spirit, you see the Father and the Son. God the Creator and Redeemer continue to exist in us through his Holy Spirit. Three-in-One. Trinity. Not three different Gods; One God, three persons. Embrace the unknowable mystery. Do not let what you don't understand about God distract you from what you do understand. God is God. We are not.

What is described is our theology but now let's look at application to daily life. The Holy Spirit has four primary roles: he is the Comforter, One who convicts us of our guilt and sin, Guide, and Sustainer of our very existence. The Holy Spirit inspired the Bible writers and opens our minds and hearts to the scriptures. The Holy Spirit draws us towards God through helping us recognize when we have gone wrong. The Holy Spirit is God, and communicates to us what he wants us to do. When you pray, the Holy Spirit is in you and responding to your deepest needs for healing. The very breath in our bodies is a gift from God through the person of the Holy Spirit that sustains our life. The Holy Spirit is the completion of "God with us, Emmanuel." The Holy Spirit is who pursues you and draws you to Jesus Christ as your Lord and Savior. The Holy Spirit is fully God.

We respond to the Holy Spirit for comfort, conviction, guidance, and sustainability and these are four significant values for being a healthy church. We can never successfully say to God, "*Stand back! We've got this! We know what to do and we're going to do it!*" All four roles of the Holy Spirit have been violated in that one statement. No, we are utterly dependent on God through the Holy Spirit for building strong, healthy Deaf Churches and Ministries. We absolutely cannot do it without being humble and watching carefully for the leadership of the Holy Spirit.

Healing and Hope

"Because of our faith, Christ has brought us into this place of undeserved privilege where we now stand, and we confidently and joyfully

> look forward to sharing God's glory. We can rejoice, too, when we run into problems and trials, for we know that they help us develop endurance. And endurance develops strength of character, and character strengthens our confident hope of salvation. And this hope will not lead to disappointment. For we know how dearly God loves us, because he has given us the Holy Spirit to fill our hearts with his love." *Romans 5:2-5*

Be a place of healing and hope

One of the reasons the importance of the Holy Spirit in the Deaf Church preceded this section, is that true healing and hope is not possible outside of the work of the Holy Spirit. Groups like AA and NA acknowledge a personal helplessness that requires dependence upon a "higher power" for sobriety. Even for those who do not know God, it is because of the goodness of God that the "higher power" is actually the Holy Spirit bringing about healing and hope. Sanctification is a religious word that means the movement from brokenness to wholeness; being made holy. But when we separate the soul into separate parts—physical, emotional, intellectual, spiritual, relational—we truncate the healing of our soul because we are ignoring or overlooking unresolved hurt. According to the Jewish way of thinking, and therefore our way, we do not *have* a soul, we *are* a soul. All of us need God's redemption and healing. We are a single being with various attributes, but of the same person. Dealing with our spirituality without addressing other areas in need of healing is inadequate and even dangerous.

We need the Holy Spirit to begin a work in us that brings healing from the past and therefore, new hope for the future. For our churches to be healthy, the people who are "the church" must be on the journey of wholeness. Come Holy Spirit. Cleanse us and heal us. Make us more into the image of our Lord Jesus Christ. We will never reach perfection because we are created beings. Only God is perfect. We are his beloved. We are called to be faithful. We are blemished as part of a fallen creation. We need healing and hope: "But you are a chosen race, a royal priesthood, a holy nation, a people for his own possession, that you may proclaim the excellencies of him who called you out of darkness into his marvelous light" (1 Peter 2:9).

Healing is not about trying harder. Healing is about letting go and trusting God. We let go of any illusion that we can fix ourselves. Let go of control issues that are the result of deep emotional injury and embrace the God of our healing, Jehovah-Rapha. Healing does not come with more effort but from responsiveness to the God who pursues us. Only God can hold us and truly take away our pain. Deaf Churches and Ministries are called to embrace the need for safe places for people to heal, whether that be in counseling, support-groups, or healthy small groups where struggling is not frowned upon. God is our healer. God gives us hope.

Mercy and Justice

> "The Spirit of the Lord God is upon me, because the Lord has anointed me to bring good news to the poor; he has sent me to bind up the brokenhearted, to proclaim liberty to the captives, and the opening of the prison to those who are bound; to proclaim the year of the Lord's favor, and the day of vengeance of our God; to comfort all who mourn…"
> *Isaiah 61:1-3a; quoted by Jesus in Luke 4:18-19.*

Reflect God's love, mercy and justice

Caring about issues of mercy and justice is one of the most prominent themes in the Bible. Micah, a prophet in the Old Testament proclaims, "The Lord God has told us what is right and what he demands:

"See that justice is done, let mercy be your first concern, and humbly obey your God" (Micah 6:8). God speaks to us through Amos: "I hate, I despise your feasts, and I take no delight in your solemn assemblies. Even though you offer me your burnt offerings and grain offerings, I will not accept them; and the peace offerings of your fattened animals, I will not look upon them. Take away from me the noise of your songs; to the melody of your harps I will not listen. But let justice roll down like waters, and righteousness like an ever-flowing stream" (Amos 5:21-24).

James, the half-brother of Jesus writes passionately: "Suppose a person claims to have faith but doesn't act on their faith. My brothers and sisters, can this kind of faith save them? Suppose a brother or a sister has no clothes or food. Suppose one of you says to them, 'Go. I hope everything turns out fine for you. Keep warm. Eat well.' And suppose you do nothing about what they really need. Then what good have you done? It is the same with faith. If it doesn't cause us to do something, it's dead. But someone will say, 'You have faith. I do good deeds.' Show me your faith that doesn't cause you to do good deeds. And I will show you my faith by the goods deeds I do. You believe there is one God. Good! Even the demons believe that. And they tremble! ...A person's body without their spirit is dead. In the same way, faith without good deeds is dead" (James 2:14-19, 26).

As followers of Jesus, his priorities become our priorities. We are his hands and feet on earth as the Holy Spirit leads us to do good works. Jesus identifies himself as the King who will in the final judgement separate people like sheep and goats for either reward or punishment based on how they treated others: "Then they also will answer, saying, 'Lord, when did we see you hungry or thirsty or a stranger or naked or sick or in prison, and did not minister to you?' Then he will answer them, saying, 'Truly, I say to you, as you did not do it to one of the least of these, you did not do it to me.' And these will go away into eternal punishment, but the righteous into eternal life" (Matt 25:44-46) Our willingness to stand up, against injustice and for those in need, matters to God.

Share Jesus

"Jesus came and told his disciples, "I have been given all authority in heaven and on earth. Therefore, go and make disciples of all the nations, baptizing them in the name of the Father and the Son and the Holy Spirit. Teach these new disciples to obey all the commands I have given you. And be sure of this: I am with you always, even to the end of the age." *Matthew 28:18-20*

Share Jesus through service and words

Biblically and historically, being an "evangelical" as one who brings good news of Jesus to others, has always been tied to charity and acts of mercy. St. Patrick brought the light of Christ to the Irish through setting up monasteries in the middle of population centers, throwing open the doors, and inviting the community in to eat. St. Francis of Assisi gave up material wealth in exchange for a simple life dedicated to the poor. He and his followers were noted for proclaiming the gospel boldly. By the way, St. Francis never did say "Preach the Gospel at all times. When necessary, use words." His actual closest quote makes this point: "It is no use walking anywhere to preach unless our walking is our preaching." He and his followers proclaimed the message of Jesus in both word and through service. The Methodist Movement in the Church of England, noted for its strong evangelical preaching and strict expectations of holy living, influenced leaders like William

Wilberforce, who championed the Slavery Abolition Act 1833 which brought an end to slavery in most of the British Empire (think of *The Salvation Army*, Mother Theresa, Dr. Martin Luther King, Jr.). The examples could go on and on, and are seen through Christendom and particularly through evangelical denominations.

God loves us, has a deep compassion for the poor, marginalized, those in prison, etc. and has provided a way for us to have new, changed lives full of meaning and purpose through the life, death, and resurrection of Jesus. We can be freed from our spiritual and emotional oppression. We are to resist all forms of oppression and marginalization of others. So, when you think of evangelism and missions in these terms, it makes sense that Apostle Paul reminds us by quoting Isaiah, "How beautiful are the feet of those who preach the good news!"

So how do we share our faith on a daily basis? Begin by showing up, and simply being kind. You are just one part of God's relentless pursuit of every individual, and particularly those who do not yet know Jesus. Even if you are brand new in your faith, *go see what God can do*. Paul writes in Colossians that the "mystery is this, Christ in us, the hope of glory" (Col 1:27). *Show up* with an expectation that God is up to something. Pray for God to give you 'new eyes' as you meet people; eyes to see them as God sees them. Simply be honest. Sharing faith is simply being honest about your journey—the good, bad, and ugly—and how Jesus is transforming your life.

CALL TO THE DEAF CHURCH

When Jesus announced his mission, he stood up to read from the book of Isaiah: "The Lord's Spirit has come to me, because he has chosen me to tell the good news to the poor. The Lord has sent me to announce freedom for prisoners, to give sight to the blind, to free everyone who suffers, and to say, 'This is the year the Lord has chosen.'"

As those specifically serving in the ministry context of Deaf churches and Deaf ministries, we call for a commitment to:

Freedom from Oppression

> "Give justice to the poor and the orphan; uphold the rights of the oppressed and the destitute. Rescue the poor and helpless; deliver them from the grasp of evil people. But these oppressors know nothing; they are so ignorant!" *Psalm 82:3-5*

Spiritual freedom from past, present, and future oppression

Oppression. This word has been thrown around a lot, and in the vernacular of American Sign Language, it lends a very real, quite obvious picture as to what it means. Oppression is nothing more than an imposed domination of another person, or a group of people in order to control them mentally, physically, emotionally, and the worst of all, spiritually. Spiritual oppression is defined on the basis of, "This is your lot in life, and there is no other recourse. You just have to accept it!" While this view is dominant, we must understand that all oppression begins in and with the perspective that operates in the marginalization of others and must be considered illegitimate. Yet, even with continued scientific advancement and accomplishment, oppression abounds, still!

Oppression is an abuse of power, or authority. Deaf people are even oppressed within their own families. Many parents refuse to recognize the personal, linguistic and cultural heritage of the Deaf

Community which is important for us to embrace and cherish. Instead, children are forcibly being made to conform to the image of the created, instead of the creator. We are not hearing people with broken ears. In reality, we are created Deaf in the image of God and called according to His good purposes.

No wonder we often find Deaf people who self-oppress or oppress others. Virtually anyone constantly fighting off the negative and erroneous statements ingrained in a distorted self-concept based on barriers instead of gifts and talents; to believe they are nothing more than what they are, to believe there is nothing more possible than to accept one's deafness as a disability is a pathway to self-oppression. But there is hope.

Christian liberty has constantly experienced a significant tension that between cultural expectations that are placed upon us and the desire to be accepted as free. Because Christ has set us free, Galatians 3:28 tells us there is no difference between "... Jew nor Greek, there is neither slave nor free, there is no male and female... [*insert Deaf, Hard of Hearing, Hearing*] ...for you are all one in Christ Jesus." We are still bound by human nature that oppresses and marginalizes those that are perceived as different. Paul insists we not abuse our freedom, but instead we should fulfill the law of Christ. Certain expectations, rules, and commands definitely embolden us to serve in building up others for the cause of Christ in the power of the Spirit through relationships of healing and hope in a personification of love, mercy and true justice of God. This is not permission to ignore or deny the injustices done to our community, but rather a clarion call and foundation for confronting and overcoming them.

Healing and Restoration

"The Lord hears his people when they call to him for help. He rescues them from all their troubles. The Lord is close to the brokenhearted; he rescues those whose spirits are crushed." *Psalm 34:17-18*

Build bridges for healing and restoration

The first sermon given by Jesus, based on Isaiah 61, reminds us "who we are" through the announcement of his purpose on earth: "The Spirit of the Lord is on me, because he has anointed me to proclaim good news to the poor. He has sent me to proclaim freedom for the prisoners and recovery of sight for the blind, to set the oppressed free, to proclaim the year of the Lord's favor" (Luke 4:18-19). Jesus came to set the captives free. Consequently, this means that it is our job as followers of Jesus—those who live according to the call, purpose and design of God—to edify and build up the body of Christ among whom the Deaf belong to be able to live in the power of this good news: true freedom is release from the spiritual and personal bondage of historic oppression and marginalization, to be able to live according to the purpose and design that God has created us.

The Apostle Paul carried on this mission for spiritual freedom. It is from Paul that we discover that spiritual freedom is a noun (*eleutheria*), a verb (*eleutheroo*) and an adjective (*eleutheros*). He reminds us that spiritual freedom is an experience to possess, today; an experience we live in, and definitely a quality of life by which we are identified and to which we are called. While it might be clear that Paul specifically uses these terms to proclaim the Gospel of Jesus Christ (as distinct from denoting a particular social status), these terms are confined to and found in letters of Galatians, Corinthians and Romans.

Nevertheless, the theme of personal *freedom* is expressed as an essential part of God's Kingdom here on earth.

In practical terms, the Deaf Church needs to become a place of healing and restoration of injured people and broken relationships. This needs to become part of our spiritual DNA that we do not *execute our wounded*. We are *all* sinners and there is no place for judgmental attitudes or behaviors but anyone other than the King himself. Loving people and embracing our ministry of reconciliation likely involves support groups, access to qualified counselors, and encouragement of emotional transformation through the power of the Holy Spirit. Being seen by the world as gossips, slanderers, and haters is our shame. Create new stories of lost people finding hope in church. We too, once were lost, but now are found. We need each other to build bridges so we can find our way home.

Resist Oppression

> "Therefore, put on every piece of God's armor so you will be able to resist the enemy in the time of evil. Then after the battle you will still be standing firm." Ephesians 6:13

Advocate against all oppression

The history of the human race, and all too often in the Christian church, is a history of discrimination between people on the basis of human preferences or human fears. This is also identified as *marginalization*. We often end up failing to acknowledge that we are creatures of the same God, and bear His image. Too often, the Church, as an institution, has failed to be the salt and light in the witness against the marginalization of individuals or groups. Either the church unknowingly participates in inequality, or lifts no hand in correcting this injustice.

While we are marginalized from the outset, it is not our destiny. Oppression is the fruit of a world broken by sin. The Kingdom we belong to is full of justice and peace into which we will be resurrected. Spreading the message of Jesus Christ and resisting injustice are not mutually exclusive as we are led to believe. In fact, they are inseparable. Spiritual freedom from and against past, present, and future oppression is part of our mission. As the prophet Amos writes, "But let justice roll down like waters and righteousness like an ever-flowing stream" (Amos 5:24). We must be examples of true justice, righteousness and freedom.

Injustice requires a response. Active prayer leads to prayerful action. As followers of Jesus, resistance to oppression always requires nonviolence. Threats, anger, viciousness, and other worldly acts of violent attitudes and behaviors is sin. Likewise, avoidance of conflict due to fear, insecurities, or need of other's approval are sin. We serve a God who is relentlessly active in our world. We never want to be complicit in the oppression of others by standing idly by. There are many productive and Christ-like ways to resist oppression but one essential principle is to act intentionally with wise council, and not just react to the oppression. Stand strong with respect, be courageous with gentleness, and keep your emotions under control. Go with others.

Our ultimate goal is not to punish, but to redeem the heart of the offender. Jesus says, "You have heard the law that says, 'Love your neighbor' and hate your enemy. But I say, love your enemies! Pray for those who persecute you! In that way, you will be acting as true children of your Father in heaven. For he gives his sunlight to both the evil and the good, and he sends rain on the just and the unjust alike" (Matthew 5:43-45).

Empowerment

> "I pray that from his glorious, unlimited resources he will empower you with inner strength through his Spirit. Then Christ will make his home in your hearts as you trust in him. Your roots will grow down into God's love and keep you strong." *Ephesians 3:16-17*

Empower the Deaf community to serve and lead

Empowerment, Leadership, Service ... it seems we need to ponder the relationship between these three words. Jesus commissioned twelve disciples to reach the world with His message. Think about this for a moment. There were men who had probably never gone more than a few hundred miles from their place of birth. They were largely uneducated and poor. They lived in world that despised them, under the oppression of Roman authorities. And yet, Jesus said, "Go into the world and make disciples of all nations" (Matthew 28:19-20).

Then, as only he could, Jesus gave them the power to do so. One only has to read through the book of Acts to see how that empowerment proceeded—from willingness to listen, to commitment to obey, to the internal residence of the Holy Spirit in their hearts, to the strengthening of the disciples to endure persecution, to the impact that was being made on those who were coming into contact with them, and the subsequent empowering of these individuals to be the Church that God would lead them to be. The disciples were being transformed to lead others into a relationship with the ONE who would be able to fix the situation through them!

When we read the scriptures, we realize that Jesus did not promise clout or influence. He did not even promise success. But he did promise "I am with you always, to the end of the age" (Matthew 28:20). Jesus was empowering His disciples through the Holy Spirit by providing the resources and creating the conditions to do what they were called to do. To be an effective servant of the Lord, we must think of empowerment, equipping others, and providing the means of freedom in order for effective leadership to be reflected. This is the way of Jesus.

Failure, contrary to the common perception of the world, is not final. Failure is instructional. Empowering others means they must have the freedom to fail, to learn and to ultimately arise from their mistakes. Like the disciples, we want to be empowered. The same Holy Spirit that empowered these disciples empowers us today to serve, lead and empower other Deaf people to be actively involved in making a change in our world. Each generation carries the responsibility to understand the faith passed to it and accurately pass on that faith to their children and children's children. Deaf leaders need to inspire, equip, and empower younger leaders to continue this conveyance of experience. This is our part of the legacy and perpetuation of the Christian faith.

Interactive Experience

"This is a time to celebrate before the Lord your God at the designated place of worship he will choose for his name to be honored. Celebrate with your sons and daughters, your male and female servants, the Levites from your towns, and the foreigners, orphans, and widows who live among you." *Deuteronomy 16:11*

Interactive fellowship, instruction, and worship

Culturally appropriate Deaf Church has always been more interactive in instruction and worship than traditional hearing churches. However, it is a fair critique to note the tendency of Deaf churches to emulate hearing churches in music and preaching. These worship dynamics are many times not the "cutting edge" of hearing patterns, but rather the previous wave of hearing church practices. The hearing church began using music videos behind music and several years later, the Deaf church picked this up. The hearing church pastors started wearing more casual attire and then eventually the Deaf church pastors did. Before you react to this observation, think about the resources and access that the hearing church enjoys that has been denied the Deaf church. It only makes sense that the Deaf churches would tend to follow behind. This observation is not to be critical but presents an opportunity to *refocus* culturally-sensitive Deaf worship (theme of the Deaf Mission's *2018 Deaf Christian Leadership Conference*) to become more intentional, creative, and contextually appropriate.

Chad Entinger, CEO of Deaf Missions, is noted as saying "Drama is to Deaf people what music is to hearing people." Should short vignettes and acting out scripture become more commonplace in Deaf Churches? Instead of announcements, signed music, scripture, and a 20-25 minute sermon (basically in that order), what would it be like to have a short skit followed by a 10-minute homily (short sermon) leading into small group discussion and concluding with sharing insights, closing comments, and pairing-off to pray? The point is not to have uniformity of a new model of Deaf Church across the world, but to become more intentional about interactive fellowship, instruction, and worship. The Deaf Church loses focus when blindly following whatever style is popular in hearing churches. There is enough creativity, innovation, and wisdom in the Deaf Community to create effective models of biblically-sound, worship communities.

At the same time, remain a student of current trends in society and culture. Always pay attention to where God has planted you and the uniqueness of your fellowship. In using a sports analogy, coach the team you have not the team you wish you had. But every team can improve and even excel if coached well. Learn from everything you see and read but remember that Deaf Church and ministry is not just about adapting hearing ministry to remove communication barriers. Build intentional, biblically-sound, culturally-appropriate Deaf churches that glorify God through a prayerful commitment to excellence in all spiritual things.

Embrace the Marginalized

> "In that day the deaf will hear words read from a book, and the blind will see through the gloom and darkness. The humble will be filled with fresh joy from the Lord. The poor will rejoice in the Holy One of Israel." *Isaiah 29:18-19*

Embrace the marginalized in both Deaf and Hearing worlds

For more than 400 years (roughly 1850-1400 BC), the people of Israel were in bondage to the government of Egypt. In Exodus 2 and 3, certain words are used that particularly denote oppression: *imposed, compelled, bitter, task master, bondage, sighed, groaning, affliction, smiting, burdens, wrong, killed, feared, sorrows,* and *cry*. Many of these and similar words describe and define the experiences of marginalization in the ancient world and are still seen regularly in today's social media.

These experiences do not reflect the kind of distinction and attitude that Jesus teaches and presents in the Sermon on the Mount where a contrast is highlighted between good and evil. Jesus firmly rebukes marginalization that expresses itself through attitudes of judgement of others based on some standard of goodness, worth and acceptability. The Christian church, as the body of Christ, must include the diversity of personalities, gifts, races, and gender. The task of the Church is mutual acceptance and unity "in the bond of peace ... until we all reach unity in the faith" (Eph. 4:3,7).

The Deaf community, even after all our educational and technological advancements, are still dramatically oppressed in society. We are oppressed—politically, economically, educationally, socially—which exhibits itself in emotional abuse and neglect with few of the supports and resources enjoyed by our hearing peers. Marginalization on the basis of disability is dealt with, rather insufficiently, on the legislative level. Yet, by and large, the Church continues to remain inactive on these issues. Furthermore, oppression within the Deaf community is prevalent on the basis of color, heritage, and language acceptance and communication.

Oppression, marginalization and social differentiation happens in all walks of life, and carries with it severe repercussions, mentally, physically and socially. But are we in the right when we marginalize the hearing? I grew up with the saying, "Two wrongs don't make a right." Jesus had followers who in others settings would have killed each other—Simon the Zealot and Matthew the Publican are the two most obvious—but he taught them to live together as brothers. To adapt a quote from Martin Luther King, Jr, promote an attitude of learning to 'judge people by the content of their character, not the decibels they can hear.' In our hearts, we know it is wrong to marginalize others. Jesus reminds his listeners at the Sermon on the Mount, "So whatever you wish that others would do to you, do also to them, for this is the Law and the Prophets" (Matt. 7:12).

Equal Accessibility

> "For you are all children of God through faith in Christ Jesus. And all who have been united with Christ in baptism have put on Christ, like putting on new clothes. There is no longer Jew or Gentile, slave or free, male and female. For you are all one in Christ Jesus. And now that you belong to Christ, you are the true children of Abraham. You are his heirs, and God's promise to Abraham belongs to you." *Galatians 3:26-29*

Consistent awareness of diverse language backgrounds to ensure the message of the gospel is equally accessible to all

Jesus, in his commandment to the disciples prior to his ascension was to, "...go, make disciples of all nations ... teaching them to obey everything I have commanded you" (Matt. 28:19-20). Peter reminds us that true, spiritual transformation does not happen without a person being actively engaged with the Word of God. "May God give you more and more grace and peace as you grow in your knowledge of God and Jesus our Lord" (2 Peter 1:2). The overwhelming challenge for the Global Deaf Community is that it represents over 400 different signed systems. Fortunately, several Christian organizations are actively translating the Bible through video into a number of different signed heart languages.

On Pentecost, the Holy Spirit miraculously allowed people from all over the world to understand God's message in their own language.

"They were completely amazed. "How can this be?" they exclaimed. "These people are all from Galilee, and yet we hear them speaking in our own native languages" (Acts 2:7-8). Consequently, on that day, the gospel began to go out into the world. Making disciples involves more than simply translating the scriptures for evangelism, spiritual growth, discipleship, and mentoring in the Christian life. All represent the process of growth that involves commitment from all of us. We must know the heart language, culture, and communication preferences to help others grow in Christ.

Although American Sign Language is the recognized native Deaf language in our country, not all deaf people sign the same way, nor even sign at all. Roughly 50% of people born deaf or hard-of-hearing never learn fluency in ASL. As part of the celebration of Deaf Awareness month in 2019, the Deafhood Foundation released a bold statement paper discouraging any continued use of the descriptor, "d/Deaf" as a way to delineate between kinds of Deaf people: "The Deafhood Foundation celebrates Deafkind by recognizing and endorsing the use of capital D for all of our people in the same way other ethnic groups capitalize the labels they use to describe themselves. We do not support the use of d/Deaf to indicate who is culturally Deaf and who is not. That creates artificial divisions in our community. The time for perpetuating those divisions in different ways, including the terms and labels we use, such as "Not Deaf enough" and "Too Deaf" are over. It is past time to come together and wholeheartedly accept the entire spectrum of Deaf people as Deaf."[75]

---

75 Deafhood Foundation, Statement on Use of d/D, accessed March 29, 2019, http://deafhood.org/news/to-d-or-not-to-d/?fbclid=IwAR3ZRISC7iY7GHXQASj-hvQnuMuUtYJbeoppYRpsMq7FF8bzRl3TjI8Ly-o

As we expect accommodations for our own communication needs, Deaf Churches and Ministries are wise to adapt to the communication needs of Deaf-Blind, Deaf Plus, Deaf Oral, and Deaf from diverse cultural backgrounds. We are compelled by the Holy Spirit to help each person understand the gospel in his or her own heart language. All God's children have a place in our family of faith, regardless of how they communicate. Everyone deserves an opportunity to make an informed decision about following Jesus.

Discussion Questions

1. Why do you think the authors began with a general call to the church to reflect certain values and priorities instead of only focusing on Deaf-specific issues? What are potential dangers in not elevating these first seven priorities?

2. In a community of *grace, unity, healing and hope*, how does correction of theological or moral error look (or even removal of someone) in practical terms?

3. Addressing issues of *oppression, marginalization, and audism* is vital but runs the risk of redefining a group's identity to one of anger and resentment; what practical ways would a church advocate without spiritual compromise?

4. What does it mean for a church to pursue *spiritual freedom from past, present, and future oppression*? Describe how a church might work to bring this about.

Deeper Dive: Who are the *marginalized* within the Deaf community? How might *both Deaf and Hearing people* experience neglect and exclusion? What are ways to be truly *inclusive* of diverse people within the church without losing a sense of outward mission? What are practical ways to *empower* the Deaf community *to serve and lead* in a hearing church while avoiding tokenism? In a Deaf Church, how is *empowerment to serve and lead* applied? Acceptance of *diverse language* preferences for equal access to the gospel in a Deaf Church is controversial in some sectors, so how does this value coexist with a commitment to Deaf Culture and American Sign Language?

CHAPTER V—Biblical Foundations

Sound theology springs forth from a healthy understanding of the biblical narrative as the ultimate authority. Jude 1:3 alerts us to protect "...our common salvation, I found it necessary to write appealing to you to contend for the faith that was once for all delivered to the saints." Christianity has been formed in various contexts and shaped by many influences over time: historical Church councils, religious discourse between nations and people groups, the Reformation, the various missionary movements, and great theological thinkers. Yet, the Christian belief system has not been significantly altered nor dissipated into oblivion; in fact, there remains a remarkable historic consistency about the fundamentals of our faith. The Holy Spirit continues to provide clarity and direction for the Church based on the Old and New Testaments.

This final chapter focuses on the biblical foundations for the Deaf Church and Deaf Ministry in the context of a highly secular society. Everything has changed, but in a sense, nothing has changed. The writer of Ecclesiastes reminds us, "What has been is what will be, and what has been done is what will be done, and there is nothing new under the sun" (1:9). The Bible is as vibrant, alive, and applicable as it ever has been. For those who have read this far, we invite you into the deepest dive yet, the foundations for our whole effort: the Holy Bible. In these pages, we hope you will rediscover the depth of your calling as one who loves the Deaf Church. As Christians, we are part of a promise that reaches back over four millennia and a legacy that will stretch far into the future. The Bible is our foundation for all who are to follow.

Redemptive Heritage

In understanding the covenantal relationship between God and his people, certain values remain consistent in the biblical narrative regardless of the paradigms used for understanding this interaction.[76] The unfolding revelation throughout biblical history reveals a pattern of God's agreement to bless a covenant community, who in response make a commitment to faithfully maintain priorities of holiness and charity, both individually and collectively. The Abrahamic Covenant is explored as foundational for the Judeo-Christian faith and a prototype for other biblical covenants. The first response of a faithful covenantal community is to offer praise and honor to God, who is both the author and sustainer of the covenant.

In response to God's goodness and power, emergence or renewal of a sacred assembly is generally the first order of business. This sacred assembly gathers to celebrate God's presence and provision. God's covenant comes with a condition of holiness for the receiving of blessing. The covenant community is "set apart" for the purposes of living distinct from those who are not part of this faith community. Remaining a holy people must include having a means of confession, forgiveness, and redemption for there to be any prospect of success. Yet the biblical narrative is brutally honest regarding the struggle of the covenant people to remain faithful over time.

76 G. Goldsworthy, "Relationship of Old Testament and New Testament" in *New Dictionary of Biblical Theology*, eds. T.D Alexander and B.S. Rosner (Downers Grove: IVP, 2000), 86-89. Goldsworthy explains a number of proposed thematic polarities for the synthesis of the scriptures such as: Old and New Covenant, Law and Gospel, Israel and the Church. In all, seven thematic polarities are presented.

The need for spiritual instruction and personal reconciliation with God and others is essential to maintain a religious community. The community does not simply reject any who fail but must establish a means of restoration. With the final atoning sacrifice and resurrection of Jesus, the covenantal community now experiences an opportunity for sustained holiness through the presence of the Holy Spirit. God's fulfillment of the Abrahamic Covenant provides a framework for understanding the essential values of the church: sacred assembly, holiness, community, mission.

The calling for the Deaf church is twofold: renewal of a faithful, biblical understanding of what it means to be church in general and a specific commitment to the distinctiveness of a linguistic and cultural ministry to the Deaf community. The "Declaration to the Deaf Church" was built upon a biblical witness of covenant, sacred assembly, holiness, community, and mission. The priority is to identify foundational components of life together as part of a faith community. Theology grounded in scripture must form and guide application of these principles or else mission drift will occur.

The Abrahamic Covenant

God's covenant with Abraham as unfolded in Genesis 12-50 presents four identifiable themes that define the relationship between God and his chosen people who serve as his vessel of salvation for the world: God would bless Abraham with many *descendants* and a new *homeland*; in response, Abraham would be *obedient* and all nations would be *blessed* through him. Not only was Abraham the patriarch of the Jewish people, he was the original source of all God would do to protect, guide, and provide for them and through them to all humanity.[77] Although there would be future covenants between God and his chosen people—such as the Mosaic and Davidic covenants—later covenants modify yet do not invalidate earlier agreements. Each covenant builds upon previous ones. The scriptural pattern remains: *God will provide, the people will respond faithfully, and through this relationship all nations will be blessed.* Unfortunately, the breakdown often occurs in the obedience of the people and the covenant falls apart. Faithfulness to this *covenant*, or the lack thereof, is what ultimately defines the relationship between God and his chosen people.

Abraham is referenced in all four gospels either as part of a genealogy, cultural identity,[78] or the presiding host along with Isaac and Jacob at the eschatological banquet (Matt. 8:5-13)[79]. This passage in Matthew's gospel tells of the Centurion who came to Jesus for healing of his servant. Jesus makes this bold and potentially troubling statement: "… many will come from east and west and recline at table with Abraham, Isaac, and Jacob in the kingdom of heaven, while the sons of the kingdom will be thrown into the outer darkness. In that place there will be weeping and gnashing of teeth" (Matt. 8:12). Jesus proclaims a reinterpreting of the Abrahamic covenant to include outsiders and exclude so-called children of Abraham.

---

77 N.L. Calvert, "Abraham," in *Dictionary of Jesus and the Gospels*, eds. J.B. Green, S. McKnight, and I.H. Marshall (Downers Grove: IVP, 1992), 3.

78 Ibid. 4-6. Calvert cites Matt. 1:1-2, 17; 3:9; 8:11; 22:32; Mark 12:26; and Luke 1:55, 73; 3:8, 34; 13:16, 28; 16:22-30; 19:9; 20:37; Abraham is referenced by Jesus ten times in John 8:31-59.

79 Unless otherwise noted, all biblical passages referenced are in the English Standard Version.

Another profound incident regarding the reinterpreting (not invalidation) of the Abraham covenant by Jesus is recorded in John 8:39-59. Following an intense drama regarding a woman caught in adultery as a means to entrap Jesus[80], this interaction escalates into a heated argument where Jesus proclaims preeminence above Abraham. In response, the furious temple crowd picked up stones to kill Jesus who then hid and fled.

Abraham serves as a model of righteousness and faith in Romans 4, Galatians 3, and Hebrews 11. Through Jesus, the consummation of the blessings of Abraham comes to fruition not only for the Jewish people, but the entire world. The promise to Abraham is fulfilled at last in Jesus. A new covenant was nearing commencement. No longer would the agreement include offspring and Promised Land, but a new spiritual family and an eternal kingdom. The intention was for the renewal of a community and not just individuals, although the two are intricately linked.[81]

While Abraham is held up as a heroic figure and patriarch of the Jewish and Christian faiths, scripture reveals a more honest picture of Abraham, showing times of weakness, deception, and fear. The Jewish perspective focuses on Abraham's faithfulness as the way to enter into a communal covenant. In Romans 4:1-25, Paul considers Abraham as wicked until redeemed by the Lord and righteousness was granted to him.[82] It stands to reason the Bible does not allow us to elevate

---

80 John 7:53-8:11. This initial interaction is not included in the earliest manuscripts. Even without including this prelude to the story, the claims made by Jesus regarding preeminence are not in question.

81 I.H. Marshall, "Church," in *Dictionary of Jesus and the Gospels*, 123.

82 Kenneth A. Mathews, *Genesis 11:27-50:26*, vol. 1B of *The New American Commentary*, ed. E Ray Clendenen and Kenneth A. Matthews (Nashville: Broadman & Holmann Publishers, 2005), 169.

Abraham to a status above that of a faithful, yet sinful man with whom God has made a covenant for saving the world.

Jesus Christ is the "founder and perfecter of our faith" (Heb. 12:2). Jesus served as the sacrificial offering to fulfill God's promise to Abraham. Like Abraham and his descendants, Christians are given the covenantal responsibility to fulfill "the promise that all the nations will now be blessed through the seed of Abraham."[83] This calling to carry forward God's plan "is a vision of *present* reality, seen in heavenly dimension."[84]

The Sacred Assembly

The biblical mandate of a covenant community is rooted in the promises to Abraham and expressed through an unfolding narrative seen throughout the Bible. God is not only calling individuals, his plan requires the obedience of the entire community for worship, mercy, and obedience. Worship as a sacred assembly holds primacy in this community as seen in Exodus and Leviticus. The Psalms provide us a hymnbook of worship; the pattern of worship seen there and elsewhere consists of praise, confession, and petitions offered in humility.[85] The prophets called for the faithful community to care for justice, fairness and mercy extended to all.[86] There is a natural connection between communal faithfulness and an individual holiness. As people who

83 N.T. Wright, *Surprised by Hope: Rethinking Heaven, the Resurrection, and the Mission of the Church* (New York: HarperCollins, 2008), 236.

84 Ibid., 281.

85 Paul House, *Old Testament Theology* (Downers Grove: InterVarsity Press, 1998), 184, 255.

86 House, *Old Testament Theology*, 190.

fully recognized their mistakes and sinful nature, the primary task was never the attainment of personal perfection as might be the case in other religions, rather the requirement was obedience. God required a humble, broken and contrite heart (i.e. Ps. 51:17; Isa. 57:15; 66:1-2). A sincere repentant attitude before a holy God is responded to by his mercy and blessings.

In the Old Testament, the presence of God was connected with a sacred place such as the tabernacle or the temple, which was made holy by the sacredness of God's presence. The dwelling place of God was originally beheld in the tabernacle as described in Exodus 36 and 40 where the "glory of the Lord filled the tabernacle" and remained "in the sight of all the house of Israel throughout all their journeys" (Exod. 40:34-38). The tabernacle was known as the "tent of meeting" or the place where heaven and earth came together. God's presence was likewise seen in the Ark of the Covenant is where these two realities overlap.[87]

In all literary forms of biblical genres—narrative, parable, poetry, wisdom, prophesy, epistles, and apocalyptic[88]—the singleness of worship of the omniscient, omnipotent, omnipresent God, who alone is worthy of praise, is paramount and non-negotiable. This monotheistic commitment to the one, true, holy God is mandatory for blessings of both the individual and the community.[89] Both the first commandment (Exod. 20:2-3, Deut. 5:6-21) and the greatest commandment (Deut. 6:4-5, Matt. 22:37, Mark 12:30, Luke 10:27) attest to this absolute

---

87 N.T. Wright, *Simply Christian: Why Christianity Makes Sense* (New York: HarperCollins, 2006), 64.

88 M. Lawrence, *Biblical Theology in the Life of the Church* (Wheaton: Crossway, 2010), 45-51.

89 House, *Old Testament Theology*, 254.

standard. God will not tolerate any competitors for loyalty and allegiance. God identifies himself as jealous and possessive (Exod. 20:5, 34:14; Num. 25:13; Deut. 4:24, 5:9, 6:15; Josh. 24:19; Ezek. 36:6, 39:25; Nah. 1:2). Faithful people honor the holiness of God through their lives as reflected in worship, devotion, generosity, and obedience.

The sacred assembly across the ages has been one of helping to recognize, and even helping to usher in, the Kingdom of God. Daniel refers to such an eschatological kingdom (Dan. 2:44) but otherwise the term itself is not used in the Old Testament, however, the idea of such a kingdom is present.[90] The image of a perpetual earthly kingdom finds traction through the Davidic era and later prophets who spoke of a future reestablishment of a faithful monarchy. This is reflected in the influential role of the prophets with monarchs such as is seen in Nathan, Gad, and Elijah.[91]

As the image of a Messiah unfolded, there were three aspects of this role: prophet, shepherd, king.[92] God unfolded this plan in and through the person of Jesus. The fullness of the proclamation and understanding of the role of the sacred assembly in relation to the kingdom of God is found in the words of Jesus himself and reflected in several epistles.[93] Revelation 11:15 proclaims, "The kingdom of the

---

90 C.C Caragounis, "Kingdom of God/Heaven," in *Dictionary of Jesus and the Gospels*, 417-30. Caragounis explains that this term, and related term "kingdom of Heaven" signify God's rule: sovereign, dynamic and eschatological. Caragounis provides several Old Testament examples of images of God as king or ascribed a royal throne or having a continuous or future reign.

91 Ibid. 418.

92 Frank Thielman, *Theology of the New Testament: A Canonical and Synthetic Approach* (Grand Rapids: Zondervan, 2005), 94-122.

93 Though some are parallel statements, fifty-four references are made to the "kingdom of God"; six in Acts, and thirteen in the epistles; Matthew adds thirty-one references to "kingdom of heaven."

world has become the kingdom of our Lord and of his Christ, and he shall reign forever and ever." Implied in the concept of this kingdom is a community where God's holiness is manifested. Scripture reveals a Jesus who saw his followers as children of God who were to share life together, gather in his name to worship, and serve others.[94] This sacred assembly is intended to be more than well-meaning, religious people. The message of Jesus' resurrection and the presence of this risen Lord in their gathering is the place of God's kingdom and lordship.[95]

The prologue to the gospel of John proclaims Jesus as the eternal *logos* of God who becomes the embodiment of grace and truth. The literary form of John 1:1-18 can be considered poetry and suggests that these words might have served as an early hymn for worship.[96] This might be an indication of the significance of this passage of scripture in poetic form or hymns as effective ways to memorize and transmit information across generations and distance.[97]

Here exists the actual fulfillment of the promise first given to Abraham. Jesus himself is the presence of God in the world and the "light and life" available to all.[98] "But to all who did receive him, who believed in his name, he gave the right to become children of God, who were born, not of blood nor of the will of the flesh nor of the will of man, but of God" (John 1:13-14). The Abrahamic covenant is now based on faith and not bloodlines. The zenith of this prologue is

---

94 I.H. Marshall, "Church" in *Dictionary of Jesus and the Gospels*, 123-4.

95 Wright, *Surprised by Hope*, 265.

96 William E. Hull, *John*, vol. 9 of *The Broadman Bible Commentary*, ed. Clifton J. Allen (Nashville: Broadman Press, 1970), 209-210.

97 Hull, 210.

98 Rodney A. Whitacre, *John*, vol. 4 of *The IVP New Testament Commentary Series*, eds. Grant R. Osborne, D. Stuart Briscoe and Haddon Robinson (Downers Grove: InterVarsity Press, 1999), 53.

found in verse 14. Jesus "became flesh and dwelt among us" revealing a life "full of grace and truth" (John 1:14). The paradigm shifts from compliance to laws to a journey of transformation, "For the law was given through Moses; grace and truth came through Jesus Christ" (John 1:17).

The holy God has now entered fully into the human experience in the person of Jesus Christ.[99] Not only did God enter the world in bodily form, he came to us as one full of grace and truth. Upon these two realities—grace and truth—the body of Christ is now to fulfill this part of the historic covenants made with God. Grace gives more than is deserves and truth reflects the trustworthiness of God's expectations.[100] An essential part of a sacred assembly is to maintain these traits in balance. Jesus models this throughout his ministry and provides several parables and teachings that emphasize these values.

Salvation is a gift of grace and not something earned. Yet behavior and works are important expressions of a heart committed to the Lord. Several passages of scripture—including the words of Jesus, his brother James, Paul, and other biblical writers—emphasize that good works are expected of those who belong to God. Jesus makes what may be his most poignant (and possibly most disturbing) point about judgment based on actions in his parable of the final judgment and the separation of the sheep and the goats (Matt. 25:31-46). Although one is saved by grace, it is foolishness to assume this implies any lack of responsibility for godly actions.

---

99 Ibid. 58.

100 Hull, *John*, 218.

In all four gospels and Acts, the divine power upon Jesus is the Holy Spirit who helps usher in the eschatological age.[101] Jesus breathes the Holy Spirit on the disciples as part of conveying his unique presence and authority (John 20:19-23). Jesus promises to be with his followers whenever they gather (Matt. 18:20; 28:20). The church exists as the present and future "body of Christ" (Rom. 7:4, 12:4-5; 1 Cor. 12:12-13, 27; Eph. 4:11-16; Col. 3:14-16) as the eschatological expression of the resurrected Jesus. The previous role of Israel as the conduit of God's grace has now been conveyed upon the church.

Jesus uses various communal images when describing his followers: little flock, city, planted field, wedding guests, family, and 'in my name.'[102] This unique expression of God in the life of Jesus empowers the church's witness, directs and disciples, ensures inclusivity, and preserves the holiness of the church.[103] In Revelation, Jesus is recognized as "heavenly priest, end-time ruler, and judge."[104] The Holy Spirit rests on Jesus Christ, visibly evidenced as a descending dove at the baptism of Jesus and at the Mount of Transfiguration. Connected with both instances is the audible voice of God the Father proclaiming how pleased he is and a command of obedience to those around Jesus. Peter testifies as an eye-witness to the second event (2 Pet. 1:16-18).

The historic covenants between God and his chosen people have now taken on a new dimension. The final sacrifice has been made. God's atonement for humanity through Jesus ascribes a new level of

---

101 Thielman, *Theology of the New Testament*, 699.

102 Marshall, "Church," 123. Cites Luke 12:32; Matt. 2:19, 3:34-35, 5:14, 13:24, 15:13; 18:20.

103 Thielman, *Theology of the New Testament*, 698-707.

104 Gregory K. Beale, *The Book of Revelation* of *The New International Greek Testament Commentary*, eds I. Howard Marshall and Donald A. Hagner (Grand Rapids: Eerdsmans, 1999), 206.

access and accountability to the faithful. His Spirit is sent to create a holy people who fulfill his purposes and marshal in a new age. It is a "new creation" that is "not simply a new religious possibility, not simply a new ethic or a new way of salvation, but a new creation."[105] This new creation is around, in, and working through believers on behalf of others. The church becomes "living stones" (1 Pet. 2:4) through the mystery of "Christ in you" (Colossians 1:27)", serving him who is the "head of the body, the church" (Colossians 1:18). The power and presence of the Holy Spirit within the sacred assembly is essential for the church for any age, in any context, and particularly for the Deaf church in reaching the next generation for Christ.

Holiness in the Kingdom of God

Faithfulness, by its very nature, draws one into the process of sanctification.[106] The call to holiness is such a clear theme within the biblical narrative that it is indisputable as part of the fulfillment of covenants with God. Historically, the acceptance of any false teachings and sexual immorality are directly related as expressions of an unwillingness to accept of God's authority. Leviticus and Deuteronomy have extensive prohibitions on idolatry and sexually immoral behavior. Proverbs repeatedly warns of the immoral woman who lures young men to certain death or destruction. The Psalms attest to the holiness of God and his majesty, sovereignty, and awesome power.[107] Paul's appeal in

105 Wright, *Surprised by Hope*, 67.

106 N.T. Wright, *After You Believe: Why Christian Character Matters* (New York: HarperCollins, 2010), 245-6.

107 David G Peterson, "Holiness," in *New Dictionary of Biblical Theology*, eds. Desmond Alexander and Brian S. Rosner (Leicester, England: Inter-Varsity Press, 2000), 545.

Romans 12:1-2 offers a succinct description of the sanctification process which results in transformed minds that discern the will of God and prove what is "good and acceptable and perfect."

God initiates salvation "while we were yet sinners" (Rom. 5:8) but does not leave us to languish in sinfulness; through his grace, he transforms us through the presence of his Spirit into the likeness of Jesus. Paul's emphasis on holiness implies an element of separation from worldly sin and fulfillment of holy living.[108] Christ is the "mediator of a new covenant, a covenant sealed with his blood" (Heb. 9:15; 12:24).[109]

As practices of the church are adapted to fit the context of a post-modern society, one cannot change this fundamental message and remain a Christian church. The atoning sacrifice of Jesus for the forgiveness of sins is as non-negotiable a Christian belief as is the resurrection. The historic creeds of the church provide a robust structure for the "faith that was once for all delivered" (Jude 3). The foundation of the church is recognition of the power of God, sinfulness of humanity, redemption made possible only through Christ, and hope for an ultimate fulfillment of the covenant in the future.[110] Scripture is to shape "faith, life, worship, and service" where the primary agenda is "to hear Scripture as the word of God."[111]

Western societies in the twenty-first century have become increasingly secularized and resemble the environments in which the early church grew. The first century was a time of an outpouring of

---

108 Ibid. 548-9.

109 R.W. Yarbrough, "Atonement," *New Dictionary of Biblical Theology*, eds. Desmond Alexander and Brian S. Rosner (Leicester, England: Inter-Varsity Press, 2000), 392.

110 Synthesis of J.Gary Millar, "The People of God," *New Dictionary of Biblical Theology*, 684-7 with Yarbrough, "Atonement," 388-92 and Peterson, "Holiness," 544-50.

111 Brian S. Rosner, "Biblical Theology," *New Dictionary of Biblical Theology*, 5.

the Holy Spirit in visible and powerful ways. In this current century, the fastest growing Christian groups worldwide are Pentecostals and Charismatics, followed by Evangelicals.[112] Of course, there is much overlap between these three groups. Jesus told his followers to depend on the power of the Holy Spirit for the right words, and Acts provides several examples.[113] The witness of the local church must be empowered by the Holy Spirit as an expression of a larger Christian tradition and community.

The responsibility of the church is to fulfill the Great Commission given by Jesus immediately before his final ascension. Power to witness is only possible if one truly embraces the promise of Jesus to be "with you always, to the end of the age" (Matthew 28:18-20). Jesus sends the Holy Spirit to make it possible for Christians to be his witnesses wherever they go (Acts 1:18).

The overarching role of the church is to create an environment for emotional, relational, and spiritual healing, as the church—the bride of Christ[114]—reaches out to lost people, welcomes them to a new life, and calls followers of Christ to a standard of living that honors God's holiness. Regardless of whether or not expressions of the Holy Spirit still exist today (i.e. speaking in tongues, healings, prophecy), it is clearly important for the Deaf church to recognize and respond to the living presence of God's spirit, particularly within secular environments.

---

112 Global Christianity – A Report on the Size and Distribution of the World's Christian Population, Center on Study of Global Christianity 2011, Pew Research Center's Forum on Religion and Public Life, accessed on August 11, 2015, http://www.pewforum.org/2011/12/19/global-christianity-exec.

113 Thielman, *Theology of the New Testament*, 702. References Matt. 10:20, Mark 13:11, Luke 12:12 and Acts 2:4, 2:11, 4:31, 6:5, 6:10, cf. 7:55.

114 Eph. 5:22-33; John 3:29; Matt. 9:15, 25:1-13; Mark 2:19, Luke 5:34; Rev. 18:23, 21:2,9; 22:17. This imagery is implied in several places in the Old Testament as well.

One of the marks of revival movements is a calling to holiness. The prophets longed for a restoration of holiness in the descendants of Israel as a "kingdom of priests and a holy nation" (Exod. 19:5-6). John's gospel emphasizes the result of sanctification as witness and mission.[115] Paul refers to the church in Ephesus under the care of Timothy as the "household of God" and as a "pillar and support of truth" (1 Tim. 3:15). Hebrews identifies the satisfaction of sacrificial covenant theology where sanctification and purification are closely associated.[116] Peter refers to followers of Christ as a "building block… a holy priesthood" who are acceptable to the Lord (1 Pet. 2:5, 9) which is reminiscent of Leviticus 11:45.[117] James 1:27 speaks of undefiled religion and visiting orphans and widows in their affliction and the importance of faith in action. Jesus sets new standards for his followers in his public sermons (Matt. 5:1–7:29; Luke 6:17-49). Paul's letters remind Christians to reveal God's character to a world who does not know God.[118] Christians on earth in all languages, including sign language, join the chorus of heavenly beings recorded in Isaiah 6:3 and Revelation 4:8b proclaiming: "Holy, holy, holy is the Lord of hosts; the whole earth is full of his glory! Holy, holy, holy, is the Lord God Almighty, who was and is and is to come!"

---

115 Peterson, "Holiness," 547.

116 Ibid. 547-8.

117 Thielman, *Theology of the New Testament*, 382.

118 Ibid. 444-5.

A Healing, Reaching Community

Pew Research Center surveyed Americans in 2012 and 19.6 percent claimed to be atheists, agnostics, or "nothing in particular"[119] According to the Barna Research Group, numbers increased to 37 percent in 2013 and 44 percent in 2015. Barna surveyed over sixty thousand people from 2008–2015 to determine the percentages of those who could be identified as post-Christian. Qualifying individuals met at least nine of fifteen criteria, such as "no belief in God, identifying as agnostic/atheist, not praying," and so forth.[120]

An earlier Barna study in 2011 surveyed the experiences people have when they do attend church. The majority of attendees had a positive sense of church involvement. Of those with negative experiences, roughly one-third of the respondents expressed they never felt a "real and personal connection" with God at church services. Half claimed no significant impact on their lives by church attendance at all.[121]

Jesus' admonition to Peter in John 21:15-17 to feed his lambs, care for his sheep, and feed his sheep applies directly to ministry in the Deaf church. Although aware that lambs are baby sheep—the natural association of this imagery being a reference to age—it is also

119 "Nones on the Rise," Pew Research Center, U.S. Census Bureau's August 2012 Current Population Survey, accessed on October 10, 2015, http://www.pewforum.org/unaffiliated/nones-on-the-rise.aspx.

120 "2015 Sees Sharp Rise in Post-Christian Population," Barna Group, accessed on October 10, 2015, https://www.barna.org/barna-update/culture/728-america-more-post-christian-than-two-years-ago#.VhOxby5VhBc. This study consisted of a random sample of 60,808 adults, ages 18 and older.

121 "What People Experience in Churches," Barna Group, January 8, 2012, accessed on June 12, 2015, https://www.barna.org/barna-update/congregations/556-what-people-experience-in-churches#.Vo1waugrKUk. This study consisted of a random sample of 1,022 adults, ages 18 and older.

appropriate to relate this image to levels of spiritual maturity. "Lambs" are the newly converted or those who may have strayed, while "sheep" are those who show evidence of a real commitment and connection with the Shepherd. The call of the pastoral shepherd is determining how to disciple these groups in the context of Deaf ministry. Lambs represent those who are either disenfranchised or run the risk of being so if proper "feeding" is not given. Sheep are those who may either stay where they are cared for and feed, or if needs are unmet, may move along to another church for better soul care.

When John Wesley established a missional community model, referred to as a Methodist "Society," he laid out several conditions for admission. His first requirement of ministry reflects the Hippocratic Oath of physicians to "do no harm," followed by "doing good." [122] Part of reaching the "lambs" of a community is to build healthy relationships for the healing process of emotional wounds incurred from early involvement in church. If ministers are insensitive to these earlier negative experiences with church, or are uncaring about the natural struggles of trying to adjust to a newly discovered personal relationship with God through Jesus Christ, harm is easily done.

The Apostle Paul refers to feeding "with milk, not solid food, for you were not ready for it" (1 Cor. 3:2), for they are still in the flesh. One cannot feed "lambs" spiritual meat or they cannot digest it. They must be cared for gently and lived among, "like a nursing mother taking care of her own children" (1 Thess. 2:7). Do no harm. Healing cannot begin until injury ceases. Christians must engage with non-believers and new believers in loving ways that are focused on the good news of

122 John Wesley, "A plain account of the people called Methodists," VI, ECCO Print Editions, reproduction from British Library, 6.

the gospel. *Love, joy, peace, patience, kindness, goodness, faithfulness, gentleness, self-control* (Gal. 5:22-23); these are the fruits of the spirit that reach lost and hurting people with the hope found in Jesus Christ.

Providing milk for lambs can be done even by younger Christians who are in earlier stages of spiritual formation but *caring for sheep* requires a higher standard and skill level. Lambs, well-fed, grow up and become more mature sheep that still need proper attention. Jesus divides the *care* and *feeding* of sheep into separate statements to Simon Peter in a way that seems to be intentional regarding the primary importance of providing pastoral care as a foundation for the instructional acts of preaching and teaching. A high percentage of people in the Barna study desired being part of "a group of people who are united in their beliefs and who take care of each other in practical ways."[123] This seems to be particularly true of the Deaf church and ministries that minister in the context of a small, tightly-knit language and cultural group.

There must be nourishment for congregations that can only come from the Holy Scriptures opened under the inspiration of the Holy Spirit: "All Scripture is breathed out by God and profitable for teaching, for reproof, for correction, and for training in righteousness, that the man of God may be complete, equipped for every good work" (2 Tim. 3:16-17). Shepherding a flock includes a willingness to teach, preach, instruct, and disciple those who are being well-cared for. But one cannot "feed sheep" a healthy spiritual diet on platitudes alone.

The prophetic role of the pastor is to be held in tandem with the pastoral role of a shepherd. Truth without grace is harmful and

---

123 "What People Experience in Churches," Barna Group.

becomes a barrier to the fullness of God. Grace without truth is incomplete and misleading. The grace Jesus brought never departed from the truth of God. Oswald Chambers reminds us to "never water down the word of God to the understanding of your people.... Hammer at it, keep at it, and drive at it, till the laziness is taken out of people's hearts and brains and bodies, and face what this Book has to say about their condition..."[124] This relational foundation allows Christian leaders to appropriately "feed the sheep" of the Lord.

History provides many examples. Martin Luther consistently refers to scripture those whom he comforts. He does so in every possible venue whether spoken, written, or proclaimed.[125] Wesley did so as well, and both he and Luther (and others) from current day perspectives may even seem overly harsh. Abandonment or dismissal of scriptural truth is an impending threat to faithful shepherding and leaves followers of Jesus spiritually malnourished.

Chambers points out an essential truth regarding the ability to provide this care: "You cannot nourish the flock of God unless you are rightly related to the Shepherd." Chambers continues, "Feeding and tending sheep is hard work, arduous work, and love for the sheep alone will not do it, you must have a consuming love for the Great Shepherd."[126]

Mature Christians must draw deeply into the presence of the Lord for this task. Ministry begins with the pastor himself or herself abiding in Christ: "for apart from me you can do nothing" (John 15:5).

---

124 Oswald Chambers, *Workmen of God* (London: Marshall, Morgan & Scott, 1975, 1937), 78-9.

125 August Nebe, *Luther as Spiritual Advisor* (Philadelphia: Lutheran Publication Society, 1894).

126 Chambers, *Workmen of God*, 87-88.

An expression of this abiding relationship is evidenced in a number of practical ways, including accountability within the context of a healthy community. Wesley writes, "strengthen you one another. Talk together as often as you can. And pray earnestly, with and for one another, that you may endure to the end, and be saved."[127] Although much can be discussed about how well Wesley actually followed his own advice, there is clearly a passion in him to experience "the image of God stamped upon the heart, inward righteousness attended with the peace of God, and joy in the Holy Ghost."[128] Wesley calls members of the Societies to "confess your faults to one another and pray for one another that you may be healed."[129] Pastoral care is an essential value for being able to share "hard-to-accept" truths to congregants.

Isolation is a dangerous threat to pastoral ministry, particularly in the Deaf church, and can often be its obliteration. Pastors of Deaf churches need to intentionally and regularly find ways to overcome seclusion. Jesus emphasized the importance of emotional, spiritual, and practical support systems for ministry in several places; likewise, Jesus modeled this for us in his relationships with the disciples and especially with his friendship with Mary, Martha, and Lazarus. Jesus spent vital time alone with the heavenly Father but also clearly shows a pattern of embracing a central group of his closest friends. At times, Jesus drew Simon Peter, James, and John—the beloved disciple—closely around him and away from the others. Jesus sent out disciples two-by-two for a reason. He spoke of his church as a community of strength against which the gates of hell could not stay closed.

---

127 Wesley, "A plain account of the people called Methodists," 5.

128 Wesley, 4.

129 Ibid. 16.

In today's world, there are other resources for the pastor to maintain a healthy marriage, receive help with parenting, encouragement from friends, guidance from counselors, insight from mentors, and refreshment through positive physical outlets. One cannot give to others what one does not possess.

Anglican Bishop Thaddeus Barnum tells of a clergyman who describes a "fortress" around his heart so he never has to really deal with people's lives and suffering. All too often this is the result of clerical training to become "doctors of the mind and not of the soul."[130] Barnum invites the reader into the "crossing"; a place where the internal and external selves meet, where people are most real. Jesus tells Simon Peter directly, and all those who are to follow in the ministry, "take care of my sheep" (John 21:16). Authenticity and transparency helps create a climate of connectivity that begins the process of overcoming isolation.

God's Vision for *Deaf Ekklesia*[131]

Koinonia[132] as a foundational understanding of the Deaf church is to be emphasized in part due to significant issues of isolation facing many deaf young adults and the need for communities of faith to provide for

130 Thaddeus Barnum, *Real Identity: Where Bible and Life Meet* (Indianapolis: Wesleyan Publishing, 2013), 31-2.

131 *Ekklesia*: (*Greek*) refers to both worldwide Church, and local body of believers. *Ekklesia* emphasizes the people as "the church" (not the building); it also provides the abstract concept of the Church everywhere. *Ekklesia* and *Koinonia* are used in this section for the purpose of showing these concepts as deeply embedded in the origins of the early Church and not just recent innovations.

132 *Koinonia*: New Testament *Greek*: deep, spiritually-based relationships within a Christian fellowship

personal healing and a sense of belonging. The four-fold priorities of gathering in Acts 2:42 are simple and easily replicated. It is reasonable to consider this model seen in Acts as the *ekklesia* appropriate for our current cultural setting. This is not intended to be the creation of a new or even recreation of an ancient model of church, but rather an effort to be true to the scriptures in the context of a highly secular culture. This perspective is an effort to encourage a faithful model of *ekklesia,* experienced as a healing, Christ-centered, and evangelical community of *koinonia* or committed Christian community.

The evidence of a healthy, faithful church is how well it is a reflection of the 'holiness of God' in the community.[133] The challenge of the Deaf church in this century is to identify the essential elements of such a model, based soundly on scriptural directives, and apply this information in a unique way for a specific population in a current context. These principles are to be applied to the specific context and challenges of Deaf churches and ministries as an expression of the larger body of Christ.

Based on these and other scriptures, it is reasonable to consider church gatherings in individual homes to be an expression of a larger Christian community but not to the exclusion of traditional church settings and venues. The priorities, based on scripture, are to create places for emotional and spiritual healing, to equip believers for knowing and sharing truth reflecting the holiness of God, and to put this faith into action in the form of service to others.

Isaiah 29:18-19 provides a unique tribute to the future inclusion of those with disabilities in the larger community of faith: "On that

---

133 Peterson, "Acts," 549-50.

day the deaf will hear words of a book, and out of their gloom and darkness the eyes of the blind will see. The afflicted also will increase their gladness in the Lord, and the needy of mankind will rejoice in the Holy One of Israel." This scripture addresses *deaf* and *blind* as part of the *afflicted* and *needy* of mankind. As the church fulfills its commitment to become the eschatological dwelling place of God, hope is restored and once again becomes the true temple of God.[134] Now to be considered: is *this* that day about which Isaiah wrote? As the prologue to the gospel of John proclaims Jesus as the embodiment of grace and truth, so Christians must become bearers of God's grace and truth as the eschatological body of Christ, fulfilling the covenant originally made with Abraham to be God's people, obedient and passionate about being a blessing to all nations.

The book of Acts provides a model of the early church that makes particular sense during a time of a rapid spread of the gospel in a largely non-Christian environment. A new spirit-filled motif of *fulfillment* is now part of God's plan for reaching all of humanity.[135] God is pouring out his Spirit in such a way for the walls of race, language, and nationality to be swept away. Acts 2:42 provides a snapshot of four priorities of the early church: apostles' teachings, fellowship, breaking of bread, and prayer. The location for this early paradigm of church occurred primarily from "house to house" (Acts 2:46, 5:42, 20:20), and lends itself to a model of church growth centered in homes. In several of Paul's letters, he specifically greets a church that meets in a home which seems to be the general pattern (Rom. 16:5; 1 Cor. 16:9; Col. 4:15; Philem 2). This precedent for house churches may be

134 Thielman, *Theology of the New Testament*, 711.

135 D.G. Peterson, "Acts" in *New Dictionary of Biblical Theology*, eds. T.D Alexander and B.S. Rosner (Downers Grove: IVP, 2000), 285-91.

especially appropriate during times of persecution, poverty, or diaspora.[136] This home-based model of *ekklesia* may be more descriptive than prescriptive but it serves as a paradigm that should be considered. Deuteronomy 6:4-9, *The Shema*, is the first part of what Jesus referred to as the greatest commandments, and emphasizes the importance of the family as the center of religious instruction for children and, by inference, the extended family and friends.

There is every indication the secularization of society will continue for now. The Millennials and younger generations—largely taught in public education settings—tend to process information and determine truth differently than previous generations. Their confidence rests primarily in personal experiences and direct observation over time. Phyllis Tickle, founding editor of the religious books department of *Publishers Weekly*, observes that enormous upheavals occur in Western civilization around every 500 years that directly impact the religious experience.[137] During these upheavals "all the other contemporaneous political, social, intellectual, and economic changes were intimately entwined with the changes in religion and religious thought."[138]

Millennials tend to distrust both the *authority* of the pre-Enlightenment and the *logic* of the Modern era. They believe that authority and logic are historic techniques for controlling and manipulating others. There is a widespread resistance among post-moderns to any

136 College of DuPage, University Bible Fellowship, accessed on May 14, 2015, www.dupage-ubf.org/documents/ConferenceMessage/House_Church_Special_Lecture_Fall09_Staff_Conference.pdf. This link no longer seems to be working.

137 Phyllis Tickle, *Emergence Christianity* (Grand Rapids: Baker Books, 2012), 17.

138 Ibid. 20.

concept of God's wrath.[139] Current secular society maintains that people are now smarter, more knowledgeable, and have the benefits of technology and science so therefore, God's ancient directives no longer apply. Implied in this mindset is that the locus of authority is not in the Bible or in any external power. Individuals become their own final authority on all matters of faith and behavior. This egocentrism, or what has previously been labeled "secular humanism," has fundamentally altered the understanding of the Christian faith, even within the church.

Though this current departure from orthodoxy is not new—the tension throughout biblical history attests to this fact—one cannot help but think of the original sin and deceptive promise that one will be like God, "knowing good and evil" (Genesis 3:5). The ancient prophets rail against false teachings, sexual perversion, and injustice to the poor. Paul addresses "works of the flesh" and false teachers in almost every epistle and notably in the Corinthian church. There is a temptation in each of the seven churches to compromise; in addition to these two mentioned, Sardis and Laodicea also succumbed.[140] When people determine to become their own source of final authority, they have turned away from God and have, in effect, become idolatrous. Hedonism and related immoral behaviors seem to be directly connected with errant beliefs used to justify these behaviors. Many in the Deaf community fall victim to negative influences which are devoid of any sense of the sacred.

In the postmodern church, we would be wise to attend to *process* as well as to *conclusion* of absolute truth. Christians need the Holy

139 Yarbrough, "Atonement," 393.

140 Beale, *The Book of Revelation*, 270.

Spirit to teach truth and direct followers as we engage non-believers within the current culture. Being directed by the Holy Spirit as to where people gather, how worship is experienced, what doctrines are embraced, and when sin is confronted is ultimately inseparable from the teachings of the church. In today's society, *how* a decision is made is often more highly valued than the perceived rightness or wrongness of the decision made. The Holy Spirit convicts believers of sin; yet, faithful Christians must show caution never to abandon truth for a goal of acceptance. As one without sin and part of the Godhead, Jesus had every right as to judge and condemn, but chose a life full of redemptive grace for those who repent. For Christians, it is wise to give careful and prayerful attention to the scriptural process of correction and rebuke (Matt. 18:15-17).

Freedom has risks, but so does legalism and oppressive religion. Jesus spoke of new wine in new wineskins but recognizes that some will prefer the old wine (Luke 5:39). The challenge of the ecclesiastical community in the twenty-first century is how to fulfill the covenant with God to be a holy people who are light in a world of darkness. James 1:27 describes undefiled religion as visiting orphans and widows in their affliction. Jesus sets new standards in the Sermon on the Mount (Matt. 5–7) and the Sermon on the Plain (Luke 6:17-49). Jesus makes what may be his most poignant point about caring for the disenfranchised in his parable of the final judgment (Matt. 25:31-46). Jesus moves the faithful from 'revenge/justice' to a 'forgiveness/redemption' paradigm of personal and social interactions with practical aspects of loving God, loving neighbor, and loving self.

There is room in the Christian faith for sincere, biblically committed followers of Christ to disagree. Paul recounts a strong disagreement with Peter over inappropriate interactions with Gentile Christians (Gal. 2:11-14). He appeals to the 'truth of the gospel' as his source of authority. Paul and Barnabas part ways with an intense dispute about Mark, yet go in peace, "commended by the brothers to the grace of the Lord" (Acts 15:39-40). The importance of unity in the church became one of the benchmarks of Paul's missionary role with conflicts being addressed in Corinth, Galatia, Philippi, and in the book of Romans.[141] Unresolved disunity is a destructive force that hurts others, and the witness of the church in the world.

Jesus commands us to love one other and Paul provides a beautiful reaffirmation of this principle in Romans 13:8-9. The current challenge is determining the application of the biblical narrative that distinguishes between the eternal truths and provisional customs and cultural milieus. Christ-centered communities of believers—who love and respect each other regardless of differences—transform the world in seminal ways. Deaf churches and ministries need to create environments where those involved witness all the fruits of the Spirit (Gal. 5:22-23).

"And Isaac dug again the wells of water that had been dug in the days of Abraham his father, which the Philistines had stopped after the death of Abraham. And he gave them the names that his father had given them" (Gen. 26:18). The wells dug by earlier generations in Deaf ministry are filled-up with new challenges faced in the context of a secular society. As the Body of Christ gathers around these concerns, those in Deaf ministry are called to strive together to offer younger generations life-giving, spiritual water. The intention of this book is to become a catalyst for change. Making systemic change requires

141 Beale, *The Book of Revelation*, 448-9.

recognizing when fundamental transition is necessary versus a general revamping of current practices.

Discussion Questions

1. The Abrahamic Covenant is a promise to become God's chosen people with certain expectations. At that point in time, what were those expectations?

2. Why is the gathering for repentance, sacrifice, and worship an important aspect of faithfulness to God? What does this look like in today's world?

3. Holiness can often gravitate into legalism. Compare and contrast holiness and legalism. John Wesley is quoted: "do no harm" followed by "do good". How have you seen both harm and good done by the church?

4. The authors emphasize the importance of building a healing community and a community that reaches out. In what situations might these priorities conflict with each other? How might they complement each other?

Deeper Dive: What is the role of *confession and repentance* in spiritual formation? In a society where historic biblical concepts are often ignored or overlooked —such as *original sin, heaven and hell, atonement for sin by Jesus' death and resurrection, and so forth* —how are new Deaf/HH converts to Christianity discipled? Explore the concept of a *Deaf Ekklesia*. What is your ideal vision of a Deaf Church to whom you will like to belong? What is the size range? How is it led? What activities occur outside of the regular worship schedule? Would it be part of a denominational structure? What is your structure for correcting *leadership* who might have become errant, ineffective, or toxic? How would this church interact and connect with other churches in your area?

ENDNOTE: Vision and Action

Ask, Seek, Knock

> "Ask, and it will be given to you; seek, and you will find; knock, and it will be opened to you" (Matt. 7:7).

DEAFCHURCH 21 is designed to elevate significant questions and create a framework for discerning pathways forward. For this to occur, people of faith need to come together to discern how 'church' might look in their communities. *Ask*, "What is your experience, what have you seen, and what makes sense to you?" In reality, ministry is 'messy' and exhausting. Give yourself permission to try new things, make mistakes, and learn from them. *Seek* a godly support system and build healthy friendships and capable mentors. Never attempt to go alone. Gather as a body of Christ, formed and led by the Spirit, for God's glory and purposes. Together, become salt and light in a world needing both. *Knock* and the door will be opened. If God is calling such a community into existence, trust that God has already prepared the way. We do not serve a God of complacency, passivity, or inaction. Our God is an always-active Creator, Savior, Sustainer and constantly innovative in the pursuit of lost people. As ambassadors of our Lord, the church offers hope and changed futures, inviting all Deaf/HH people into a community of faith, centered on Christ, and welcoming to all who sincerely respond.

If you are a **pastor or ministry leader**, with years of experience but frustrated with the seemingly endless cycle of growth and decline, drama and conflict, hope and despair, friendship and isolation; what encouragement can be offered? Don't give up. Consider the challenges identified, values elevated, and calls expressed within the *Declaration to the Deaf Church*. Ask the hard questions: "What am I (and we) doing that needs to change? Is God leading us to completely revamp how we experience 'church' or simply refocus?" *DEAFCHURCH 21* was written to provide a *compass* to guide your way and *gyroscope* for keeping your ship balanced. Please know that your sacrifice, passion for Christ, love of your congregants, and response to God's calling into Deaf ministry is greatly honored and appreciated. We praise God for you!

If you are in a **Bible study or prayer group** discerning what form your fellowship or ministry might take, stay on track with what God is doing in your hearts. Take this journey with others desiring Deaf *Ekklesia* and *Koinonia*: prayer, worship, instruction, fellowship, and service. *DEAFCHURCH 21* was written to encourage you to make your journey a mix of spiritual conversations punctuated with practical experiences of renewal—whether through lifting up the name of Jesus in worship, meeting for prayer, or serving in a homeless shelter. God has put this passion in your hearts for a reason and offers a future beyond what you can even dream or imagine. We praise God for you!

If you are a **Deaf Studies or Deaf Ministry student** reading this work as a textbook, this challenge is offered: "In what ways have your perspectives been impacted as a result of the information presented?" Excellent students are lifelong learners who continue to grow and stretch for comprehension. Learning prepares learners for even greater insights in a lifelong process that God can use to transform us more into the image of Christ. *DEAFCHURCH 21* is intended to challenge your perceptions of Deaf Church and ministry, and call you to a deeper experience of life and faith celebrated as *mystery*—Christ in us, the hope of glory. The Holy Spirit is your true guide; we pray you are constantly reminded of this reality. We praise God for you!

This generation of **youth and young adult Deaf Christians** is one of the best educated, well-informed, highly motivated, and creative groups of young people in several decades, but represents a small percentage of the overall Deaf Community. There is still much to do. Be of good faith; you are highly capable of overcoming the challenges as they arise. The *DEAFCHURCH 21* authors offer this advice: 'Ask, Seek, Knock, and the door will be opened.' Pay attention to the wisdom and lessons of the past, but do not be limited by them. Know your history so pitfalls can be avoided. Pray to the Lord of the harvest to send workers into the field, who will journey with you in your Deaf *Ekklesia*. We praise God for you!

Deaf ministry exists as a microcosm of the full spectrum of our society. This unique linguistic/cultural group requires specialized skills for reaching and incorporating new converts into the fullness of the church life. Is it a matter of simply improving what is currently being done or is there a more dramatic paradigm shift required? What are the best ways to *inspire*, *equip*, and *empower* these next generations in your community?

Ask, and it will be given to you.

Seek, and you will find.

Knock, and it will be opened to you.

"Now to him who is able to do far more abundantly than all that we ask or think, according to the power at work within us, to him be glory in the church and in Christ Jesus throughout all generations, forever and ever. Amen" (Ephesians 3:20-21).

A&M Books - Excellence in Deaf Ministry Resources

For many years, Deaf Ministry leaders have struggled for lack of adequate and credible publications in the fields of theology and practical ministry. Secular academic researchers and resources have generally neglected the role and impact of religion within the Deaf community. This publishing company is established for the purpose of creating more excellent academic resources for students and scholars in the field of Deaf Ministry. "Story" is an essential element of exploring the culture, language, and history of every people group including those who are part of the Deaf community. Developing a more comprehensive appreciation and understanding of theology and practical ministry includes the use of personal stories from within the community. Ayres & McClain Publishing creates a venue for shared stories of personal faith and the spiritual components of Deafhood.

Theological Perspective

Ayres & McClain Publishing holds to the historic tenants of the Christian faith as expressed in the creeds and based on the Bible as the final authority in all matters of belief. We are a Christian publisher that appreciates all orthodox traditions of the undivided and later reformed Church. As part of our commitment to academic integrity, there may be ideas expressed and explored by authors that the publishers do not agree with, but are found worthy of intellectual and theological consideration.

Ayres & McClain
PUBLISHING

Bibliography

Historic and Theological Foundations

Gregory K. Beale. *The Book of Revelation. The New International Greek Testament Commentary*, edited by I. Howard Marshall and Donald A. Hagner. Grand Rapids: Eerdsmans Publishing, 1999.

Broesterhuizen, Marcel. "Faith in Deaf Culture." *Journal of Theological Studies* 66, no. 2 (June 2005): 304-329. Accessed March 14, 2015. https://lirias.kuleuven.be/ bitstream/123456789/117556/1/faith+in+deaf+-culture.pdf.

Calvert, Nancy L. "Abraham." In *Dictionary of Jesus and the Gospels*, edited by Joel B. Green and Scot McKnight, 3-7. Downers Grove: InterVarsity Press, 1992.

Caragounis, Chrys C. "Kingdom of God/Heaven." In *Dictionary of Jesus and the Gospels*, edited by Joel B. Green and Scot McKnight, 417-430. Downers Grove: InterVarsity Press, 1992.

Goldsworthy, Graeme L. "Relationship of Old Testament and New Testament." *New Dictionary of Biblical Theology*, edited by T. Desmond Alexander and Brian S. Rosner. Downers Grove: InterVarsity Press, 2000.

House, Paul R. *Old Testament Theology*. Downers Grove: InterVarsity Press, 1998.

William E. Hull. *John*. Vol. 9 of *The Broadman Bible Commentary*, edited by Clifton J. Allen,189-376. Nashville: Broadman Press, 1970.

Lawrence, Michael. *Biblical Theology in the Life of the Church*. Wheaton: Crossway, 2010.

Marshall, I. Howard. "Church." In *Dictionary of Jesus and the Gospels*, edited by Joel B. Green and Scot McKnight, 122-125. Downers Grove: InterVarsity Press, 1992.

Kenneth A. Mathews. *Genesis 11:27-50:26*. Vol. 1B of *The New American Commentary*. Nashville: Broadman & Holmann Publishers, 2005.

Millar, J. Gary. "People of God." In *New Dictionary of Biblical Theology*, edited by T. Desmond Alexander and Brian S. Rosner, 684-687. Downers Grove: InterVarsity Press, 2000.

Peterson, David G. "Acts." In *New Dictionary of Biblical Theology*, edited by T. Desmond Alexander and Brian S. Rosner, 285-291. Downers Grove: InterVarsity Press, 2000.

Rosner, Brian S. "Biblical Theology." In *New Dictionary of Biblical Theology*, edited by T. Desmond Alexander and Brian S. Rosner, 3-11. Downers Grove: InterVarsity Press, 2000.

Thielman, Frank. *Theology of the New Testament*. Grand Rapids: Zondervan, 2005.

Walls, Andrew F. *The Missionary Movement in Christian History: Studies in the Transmission of Faith*. New York: Orbis Books, 1996.

Webster, Douglas D. *Living in Tension: A Theology of Ministry*. 2 vols. Eugene, OR: Cascade Books. 2012.

Rodney A. Whitacre. *John*. Vol. 4 of *The IVP New Testament Commentary Series*, edited by Grant R. Osborne, D. Stuart Briscoe and Haddon Robbinson. Downers Grove: InterVarsity Press, 1999.

Wright, N. Thomas. *Surprised by Hope: Rethinking Heaven, the Resurrection, and the Mission of the Church*. New York: HarperCollins, 2008.

__________. *Simply Christian: Why Christianity Makes Sense.* New York: HarperCollins, 2006.

Yarbrough, Robert W. "Atonement." In *New Dictionary of Biblical Theology*, edited by T. Desmond Alexander and Brian S. Rosner, 388-393. Downers Grove: InterVarsity Press, 2000.

Church Leadership and Spiritual Formation

Barnum, Thaddeus. *Real Identity: Where Bible and Life Meet.* Indianapolis: Wesleyan Publishing House, 2013

Bonhoeffer, Dietrich. *Creation and Fall: Temptation.* Touchstone ed. New York: Simon & Schuster, 1997.

__________. *Life Together.* Translated by John W. Doberstein. San Francisco: HarperSanFrancisco, [1993], 1954.

Chambers, Oswald. *Workmen of God.* London: Marshall, Morgan & Scott, 1975, 1937.

Chang, Patricia. "Assessing the Clergy Supply in the 21st Century." Pulpit and Pew Research Reports. Durham, N.C.: Duke Divinity School, 2004, accessed June 12, 2015. http://faithcommunitiestoday.org/sites/all/themes/pulpitandpew/files /ClergySupply.pdf .

Geoffrion, Timothy C. *The Spirit-Led Leader: Nine Leadership Practices and Soul Principles.* Herndon, VA: The Alban Institute, 2005.

Grounds, Vernon. "Faith for Failure: A Meditation on Motivation for Ministry."—*TSF Bulletin,* (March-April 1986): 4-6.

Harkness, Allan. "De-schooling the Theological Seminary: An Appropriate Paradigm for Effective Ministerial Formation." *Teaching Theology & Religion* 4, no. 3 (October 2001): 141-154. Accessed June 12, 2015. http://eds.b.ebscohost.com. ezproxy.samford.edu/eds/

pdfviewer/pdfviewer?vid=2&sid=71dbd774-ccf1-47ef-91ae-9d665b9af11c%40sessionmgr111&hid=108.

Herrington, Jim, Robert Creech, and Trisha Taylor. *The Leader's Journey: Accepting the Call to Personal and Congregational Transformation*. San Francisco: Jossey-Bass, 2003.

Jones, Keith G. "Towards a Model of Mission for Gathering, Intentional, Convictional Koinonia." *Journal of European Baptist Studies* 4, no.2 (January 2004): 5-13. Accessed June 12, 2015. http://eds.b.ebscohost.com.ezproxy.samford.edu/ eds/pdfviewer/pdfviewer?vid=4&sid=71dbd774-ccf1-47ef-91ae-9d665b9af11c%40sessionmgr111&hid=108.

Jones, L. Gregory, and Kevin R. Armstrong. *Resurrecting Excellence*. Grand Rapids: William B. Eerdmans Publishing Company, 2006.

Keller, Timothy. *Center Church: Doing Balanced, Gospel-Centered Ministry in Your City*. Grand Rapids: Zondervan, 2012.

__________. *Every Good Endeavor: Connecting Your Work to God's Work*. New York: Dutton, 2012.

Kelly-Gangi, Carol, ed. *Pope Francis, His Essential Wisdom*. New York: Fall River Press, 2014.

McCallum, Dennis *Members of One Another: How to Build a Biblical Ethos Into Your Church*. Columbus, OH: New Paradigm, 2010.

McCallum, Dennis, and Jessica Lowery. *Organic Discipleship: Mentoring Others Into Spiritual Maturity and Leadership*. Columbus, OH: New Paradigm, 2012.

Murray, Andrew. *Humility*. Minneapolis: Bethany House, 2001.

Peterson, Eugene H. "Lashed to the Mast." *Leadership Journal* 17, no.1 (Winter 1996): 54-60.

__________. *Practice Resurrection: A Conversation On Growing up in Christ*. Grand Rapids: William B. Eerdmans, 2010.

Sanders, J. Oswald. *Spiritual Leadership: Principles of Excellence for Every Believer.* Chicago: Moody Publishers, 2007.

Sparks, Paul, Tim Soerens, and Dwight J. Friesen. *The New Parish: How Neighborhood Churches Are Transforming Mission, Discipleship and Community*. Downers Grove: IVP Books, 2014.

Spener, Philip Jacob. *Pia Desideria: Heartfelt Desire for a God-pleasing Reform of the true Evangelical Church, Together with Several Simple Christian Proposals Looking Toward this End.* Edited by Theodore G. Tappert. Minneapolis: Fortress Press, 1964.

Stewart, Kristin. "Keeping Your Pastor: An Emerging Challenge." *Journal for the Liberal Arts and Sciences* 13, no. 3 (Summer 2009), 112-127.

Stott, John. *The Living Church: Convictions of a Lifelong Pastor.* Nottingham: IVP Books, 2011.

Taunton, Larry. "Listening to Young Atheist, Lessons for a Stronger Christianity." *Washington: Atlantic Magazine Online*, June 6, 2013. Accessed June 12, 2015, http://www.theatlantic.com/national/archive/2013/06/listening-to-young-atheists-lessons-for-a-stronger-christianity/276584/.

Webster, Douglas D. *Soulcraft: How God Shapes Us Through Relationships*. Downers Grove: InterVarsity Press, 1999.

Williams, Brian A. *The Potter's Rib*. Vancouver, BC: Regent College Publishing, 2005.

Wright, N. Thomas. *After You Believe: Why Christian Character Matters*. New York: HarperCollins, 2010.

Deaf, Millennials, and Cross-Cultural Ministry

Addison, Steve. *Movements That Change the World: Five Keys to Spreading the Gospel.* Downers Grove: IVP Books, 2011.

Ayres, Robert E. *Deaf Diaspora: The Third Wave of Deaf Ministry.* Lincoln, NE: iUniverse, 2004.

Clark, Chap. *Hurt 2.0: Inside the World of Today's Teenagers.* Grand Rapids: Baker Academic, 2004, 2011.

Connor, Benjamin T. *Disabling Mission, Enabling Witness: Exploring Missiology Through the Lens of Disability Studies.* Downers Grove: IVP Academic, 2017.

Costello, Elaine. *Religious Signing.* Toronto: Bantam Books, 1986.

Elmer, Duane. *Cross-Cultural Connections: Stepping Out and Fitting In Around the World.* Downers Grove: IVP Academic, 2002.

Evans, Tony. *Oneness Embraced.* Chicago: Moody Publishers, 2011.

Fletcher-Carter, R. and Doris Paez. "Exploring the Personal Cultures of Rural Deaf/Hard of Hearing Students." *Rural Special Education Quarterly* 29, no. 2 (Summer 2010): 18-24. Accessed June 10, 2015. http://eds.b.ebscohost.com. ezproxy.samford.edu/eds/pdfviewer/pdfviewer?vid=2&sid=1fb43ddb-e835-4063-bd33-fdf8872f5835%40sessionmgr120&hid=108.

Gannon, Jack. *Deaf Heritage: A Narrative History of Deaf America.* Silver Springs: National Association of the Deaf, 1981.

Hamill, Alexis C., and Catherine H. Stein. "Culture and Empowerment in the Deaf Community: An Analysis of Internet Weblogs." *Journal of Community & Applied Social Psychology* 21, no. 5 (Sept/Oct 2011): 388-406. Accessed June 10, 2015. http://eds.b.ebscohost.com.ezproxy.samford.edu/eds/pdfviewer/pdfviewer?vid=1&sid=78235f3c-6ceb-4708-91d3-3d944a478c91%40sessionmgr113&hid=108.

Henderson, Jim, Todd D. Hunter, and Craig Spinks. *The Outsider Interviews: A New Generation Speaks Out On Christianity*. Grand Rapids: BakerBooks, 2010.

Keuss, Jeff. *Blur: A New Paradigm for Understanding Youth Culture.* Grand Rapids: Zondervan, 2014.

Kinnaman, David, and Gabe Lyons. *Unchristian: What a New Generation Really Thinks About Christianity and Why It Matters.* Grand Rapids: Baker Books, 2007.

Ladd, Paddy, and Harlan Lane. "Deaf Ethnicity, Deafhood, and Their Relationship." *Sign Language Studies* 13, no. 4 (Summer 2013): 565-579. Accessed June 10, 2015. http://eds.b.ebscohost.com.ezproxy.samford.edu/eds/pdfviewer/pdfviewer?vid=3&sid=78235f3c-6ceb-4708-91d3-3d944a478c91%40sessionmgr113&hid=108.

Ladd, Paddy. *Understanding Deaf Culture: In Search of Deafhood.* Clevedon, England: Multilingual Matters, 2003.

Lingenfelter, Sherwood, and Marvin K. Mayers. *Ministering Cross-Culturally: An Incarnational Model for Personal Relationships.* 2nd ed. Grand Rapids: Baker Academic, 1986, 2003.

Loritts, Bryan C., ed. *Letters to a Birmingham Jail: A Response to the Words and Dreams of Dr. Martin Luther King, Jr.* Chicago: Moody Publishers, 2014.

__________. *Right Color, Wrong Culture: A Leadership Fable*. Chicago: Moody Publishers, 2014.

Lytch, Carol E. *Choosing Church: What Makes a Difference for Teens.* Louisville: Westminster John Knox Press, 2004.

Nouwen, Henri. *In the Name of Jesus: Reflections on Christian Leadership*. New York: Crossroad, 1989.

Park, Min Seo. "Deaf Culture and Deaf Church: Considerations for Pastoral Ministry." *New Theology Review* 22, no. 4 (November 2009): 26-35. Accessed June 10, 2015. http://newtheologyreview.org/index.php/ntr/article/viewFile/812/998.

Putman, Jim. *Church Is a Team Sport: A Championship Strategy for Doing Ministry Together*. Grand Rapids: Baker Books, 2008.

Putman, Jim, and Bobby Harrington. *Discipleshift: Five Steps That Help Your Church to Make Disciples Who Make Disciples*. Exponential Series. Grand Rapids: Zondervan, 2013.

Senter, Mark H., ed. *Four Views of Youth Ministry and the Church*. Grand Rapids: Zondervan, 2001.

Rah, Soong-Chan. *The Next Evangelicalism: Releasing the Church from Western Cultural Captivity*. Downers Grove: IVP Books, 2009.

Rée, Jonathan. *I See a Voice: Deafness, Language, and the Senses--a Philosophical History*. New York: Holt and Company, 1999.

Silverstone, Barbara. *The Lighthouse Handbook On Vision Impairment and Vision Rehabilitation*. Vol. 1. Oxford: Oxford University Press, 2000.

Smith, Christian, and Melinda L. Denton. *Soul Searching: The Religious and Spiritual Lives of American Teenagers*. New York: Oxford University Press, 2005.

Tickle, Phyllis. *Emergence Christianity*. Grand Rapids: Baker Books, 2012.

Van Cleve, John V., and Barry A. Crouch. *A Place of Their Own: Creating the Deaf Community in America*. Washington, D.C.: Gallaudet University Press, 1989.

Wraight, David. *The Next Wave: Empowering the Generation that will Change our World*. Colorado Springs: NavPress, 2007.